AI and the Future of Financial Planning

AI and the Future of Financial Planning

How AI will reshape wealth creation globally

Eleanor Vale

Mindful Pages

Published in 2025

ISBN: 9789371779524 (PB)
ISBN: 9789371770750(eBook)

Published by

Mindful Pages
Imprint of Alpha Editions LLC
312 W. 2nd St #1834
Casper, WY 82601, USA

This book was developed using advanced writing tools to support the drafting and ideation process. All content has been thoughtfully curated, refined, and reviewed to ensure quality and relevance.

Content

Introduction
The Algorithm and the Archetype

We find ourselves at a hushed threshold. No headlines herald its arrival, no celebrations mark the shift. Yet in the smallest motions of daily finance—the dip of a card, the quiet nod of a mortgage approval—something unprecedented is unfolding. The very fabric of financial planning is being recast. And not simply through faster sums, but through minds: algorithms, yes, but also the values, expectations, and assumptions we allow them to embody. In short, through us.

This is not the tired story of digitisation. That tale was written decades ago, when calculators replaced ledgers, and banking portals replaced the teller's counter. What we now enter is of another order entirely: the Age of Cognitive Capital. Wealth, once tethered to possessions, is increasingly measured in our ability to grasp, forecast, and—most daringly—delegate to systems that learn, interpret, and act. Intelligence itself, not just information, has become the dominant currency of prosperity.

For centuries, the craft of financial planning has rested on a familiar set of tools: common-sense rules, heuristic shortcuts, and trusted advisers. Save here, invest there, retire when ready. It was a choreography between probability and possibility, between what could be known and what could only be hoped for. Artificial intelligence changes the rhythm. It doesn't merely compute at speed; it interprets patterns, absorbs habits, adjusts to our quirks, and, increasingly, shapes the very preferences it claims to serve. Out of this emerges a new figure in the economic landscape—neither wholly human nor entirely machine—that is altering our notions of money, value, and even the future itself.

We live in a world where a teenager's phone hosts simulations once reserved for hedge funds. Where a household need not ask for advice because the assistant on the counter already knows. Where credit decisions are rendered with more accuracy than any underwriter could manage, though with a level of opacity no legal system would tolerate. The intimate act of financial planning, once grounded in conversations about trust, values, and aspirations, now risks being reduced to an optimisation puzzle solved silently in the background—often without our awareness, let alone our consent.

This book is not a technical how-to. You will not find code for robo-advisers, nor predictions of which start-up will next disrupt the markets. Its ambition is larger: to uncover the philosophical, cultural, and psychological roots of financial planning at a time when the very meaning of the practice is unsettled. We ask not just how AI will alter wealth, but why it matters, whom it serves, and what it reveals about us.

For at its core, financial planning has always been a meditation on time, identity, risk, and reward. To think about money is to wrestle with hopes and anxieties, with inherited wisdom and evolving desires. Wealth has never been only about numbers on a ledger. It has always been a proxy—safety for some, freedom for others, power, love, or all of these entwined. Now, as we place more of our choices in the hands of machines, we must wonder: do we relinquish mere arithmetic, or something closer to authorship over our own lives?

To see the magnitude of the change, one must look back. For most of human history, wealth equated to survival. Scarcity made accumulation rational—grain, livestock, gold, all guarded against uncertainty. With stability came strategy. Investment, once foreign, became a way to build, not merely to protect; to shape futures, not simply endure them. Insurance, pensions, and diversified portfolios transformed raw uncertainty into navigable risk.

Artificial intelligence marks a new turning point—one rooted not in markets but in cognition. Traditional finance assumed humans, flawed though they were, remained ultimate decision-makers. AI unsettles this assumption. It creates actors capable of modelling feelings, simulating trust, and issuing judgements independent of us. Such a shift forces us to reconsider the identity of the financial planner. What does it mean to plan when the "planner" is no longer human? And where lies accountability when decisions are optimised in ways even their designers struggle to explain?

These questions are hardly academic indulgence. They form the front line of ethical and economic debate. The rise of ambient finance—systems running quietly in the background, nudging and steering—demands urgency. Who determines the objectives these systems pursue? Whose values find their way into their code? When an app congratulates you for skipping a coffee, is it saving you, or training you? When an algorithm sidelines your long-term aspirations because your short-term habits suggest weakness, is it wise—or intrusive?

This, then, is our terrain. The reason for this inquiry, and for its timing. The stakes are not confined to technology. They reach into our sense of responsibility, our definition of prudence, our vision of what it means to be financially wise. When machines can out-plan us, the question is no longer whether optimisation is possible—but whether it is desirable. And if it is, to what end?

In the chapters ahead, expect provocations as well as analysis. You will revisit the familiar characters of finance—savers, spenders, investors—viewed through a new prism. You will see how desire itself bends under the influence of personalised nudges, and how the currency of attention is emerging as a capital in its own right. The adviser, too, must be reimagined—not as calculator, but as interpreter of opaque outputs, a counsellor rather than a broker. And you will be asked to envision models of wealth that stretch beyond borders, currencies, or even individual ownership.

At its heart, this is a book about power—yes, the power of AI, but also the power of choice. About trust—not only in machines, but in our own judgement and the institutions we construct. About value—not merely what can be tallied, but what resists measurement. And, ultimately, about legacy—not as paperwork, but as lived meaning.

What we face is not a crude battle of humans versus machines. It is, instead, a rare opportunity: to design a financial future that balances precision with purpose, autonomy with empathy, efficiency with ethics. To bring the algorithm into dialogue with the archetype.

If we meet this challenge with curiosity and courage, AI need not be our successor but our reflection. Not a master to obey, but a mirror to study. Not the end of financial planning, but its reinvention—one richer in questions, fuller in conversation, and more human in intention than ever before.

So let us begin.

Chapter 1
The Silent Revolution of Financial Intelligence

Once, the path of finance was visible enough to be walked. Its structure was laid brick by brick on intuition, ledgers, calculators, and calendars dotted with tax deadlines. The logic had a rhythm: sequential, sometimes obscure, yet within reach. Whether you were an employee setting aside funds for retirement or a business owner hedging against risk, the tools felt built for human use. Advice was offered in person, choices were deliberate, and, at least on the surface, the client remained in command.

That world is dissolving—not with fanfare, but almost inaudibly.

History's most consequential upheavals rarely announce themselves. They creep forward quietly, reshaping life until the familiar is not merely outdated but unrecognisable. Such is the state of financial planning today. At first glance, the shift looks technical—an upgrade from spreadsheets to smart apps, from wall calendars to automated alerts. But beneath that polish lies something weightier: the move from automation to autonomy. Machines are not just carrying out orders anymore; they are offering advice, predicting behaviours, correcting missteps, and optimising futures. In short, the tools are beginning to think—and often with more acuity than we manage ourselves.

This chapter considers a revolution so subtle it disguises itself as convenience. Its language is not manifestos but push notifications and nudges. Yet its implications reach far. The capacity to plan and manage wealth, once the exclusive domain of human reason, is increasingly shared with, delegated to, or even displaced by machines. This is not automation in the classic sense. Automation follows rules. Autonomy interprets them, adapts them, and at times rewrites them altogether. The distinction is more than semantic.

When ATMs replaced bank tellers, that was automation: the same sequence of tasks moved from humans to machines. Deposit, withdraw, confirm—each still required our explicit input. Now we face a different creature altogether: machine-learning models that anticipate, detect, and adapt. Financial tools no longer sit passively, awaiting instruction; they evolve into advisors. They memorise habits, decode goals, and recalibrate based on patterns we ourselves may fail to perceive.

The consequence is a reordering of the adviser–client bond. Historically, that bond was conversational: data infused with trust, numbers tempered by story. The adviser gathered details, asked questions, projected outcomes, and counselled decisions. But what happens when an algorithm consumes years of transaction data, compares it to millions of behavioural profiles, and offers guidance in an instant? Who commands greater trust—the human seen once a quarter, or the system that responds daily, even hourly?

This is not a purely technical dilemma. It is emotional, relational, even philosophical. What does it mean to be counselled by something that has no emotions yet reads yours with unnerving precision? What becomes of the authority of spreadsheets when overshadowed by the behavioural analytics humming quietly behind the interface? These are not academic curiosities. They are threshold questions for a new era, where financial intelligence is ambient—everywhere, invisible, and deeply embedded.

Think of the middleman's long reign. For centuries, intermediaries were indispensable: brokers, underwriters, managers. Their advantage lay in access and expertise—they knew what you did not, and they acted in your stead. That moat is crumbling. With a smartphone, a teenager can now glimpse the algorithmic insights once hoarded by hedge funds. Retail investors, through AI-driven platforms, can build portfolios, model scenarios, and adjust risks on the fly, without speaking to a soul in a suit.

But disintermediation is not just about cutting costs or streamlining. It alters literacy itself. The gulf between amateur and professional narrows, not because amateurs are learning more, but because the system learns for them. Complexity is hidden behind design.

Intricate models are condensed into dashboards, decisions into sliders and swipes. Participation in finance becomes seamless, but also strangely detached from deliberation.

With this access comes a paradox. Greater control may coexist with diminished awareness. Invisible planning—where systems save, rebalance, and adjust behind the scenes—creates a kind of financial autopilot. Many users are no longer planning; they are being planned for. At first, the appeal is obvious. Why not let an intelligent system handle the tedious bits? But lurking beneath is a disquieting question: when choices are ambient, what becomes of agency?

Agency, after all, is more than action. It is the awareness of options, the pause for reflection, the acceptance of consequence. When an app reshuffles spending categories or quietly alters risk levels, who is in charge? The user, or the system? Consent grows slippery. Was it granted once, long ago, buried in terms of service? Was it ever fully understood? Is the choice real, or an engineered default masquerading as personalisation?

These tensions are not speculative. They play out daily in the subtle mechanisms of ambient finance: round-up savings features, AI-driven credit scoring, behavioural risk flags, dynamically priced mortgages. To most, these appear as ease. Yet ease is not comprehension. And in finance, comprehension is not optional; it is foundational to empowerment.

Then comes the matter of data. The reigning faith is simple: more data, better outcomes. Quantify, model, predict—and optimisation will follow. It is a seductive belief, yet a fragile one. Human lives are not spreadsheets. They are riddled with contradictions, shaped by culture and emotion. Algorithms cannot weigh the guilt of inheritance, the sting of debt, the pride in generosity. They cannot balance the yearning for security with the gamble of fulfilment, nor compute the psychic cost of a safe job against the liberation of autonomy.

This limitation matters. When we trust machines to optimise, we implicitly accept their assumptions about what counts. An algorithm maximising returns will guide us toward behaviours aligned with that metric, whether or not they align with our values. Historical data, once coded, can perpetuate historical inequities. The machine's "intelligence" is never neutral; it is freighted with worldview, embedded not in text but in weights, biases, and probabilities.

To navigate such terrain, technical literacy is insufficient. What we need is conceptual clarity. We must learn to read machine outputs for their hidden assumptions, not merely their surface utility. We must act as interpreters as much as users. And we must cultivate a form of financial intelligence that marries human discernment with machine precision—aware that while wisdom cannot be programmed, it must still guide our choices.

This chapter, then, is an invitation. You will explore the difference between automation and autonomy—not as software jargon, but as a philosophical divide. You will trace the fading of the middleman, not as efficiency, but as socio-economic recalibration. You will enter the terrain of ambient finance, where convenience rubs against questions of consent. And you will confront the limits of quantification—not to dismiss data, but to rehumanise how we interpret it.

The revolution of financial intelligence is already in motion, quiet yet inexorable. The issue is not whether we take part, but whether we do so awake, questioning, creative. The systems are learning. The tools are humming. The intermediaries are slipping away. The plans continue, silently, in the background. But meaning—real meaning—still requires a human hand to write it.

So let us begin again, by learning how to see.

From Automation to Autonomy

In financial services, the distinction between *automation* and *autonomy* is not semantic—it is foundational. One executes; the other decides. One follows logic; the other learns from context. As artificial intelligence becomes embedded in the fabric of financial planning, this shift—subtle to the casual observer—has begun to rewire the advisor-client relationship from its roots. Where once technology served as a silent assistant, it now emerges as a strategic actor, capable of influencing decisions, anticipating needs, and, increasingly, shaping behaviour. This is not simply a transformation in tools—it is a transformation in trust, authority, and human agency.

Traditional automation in finance has long been defined by rule-based execution. Direct debits, payroll systems, tax calculations—these are the sterile domains of structured inputs and predictable outcomes. They are dependable, efficient, and fundamentally inert. Even more recent developments such as robo-advisors in their earliest iterations—basic portfolio balancers based on Modern Portfolio Theory—were essentially linear systems, guided by pre-set heuristics and rebalancing schedules. These systems *performed* finance; they did not *understand* it.

Autonomy introduces a different architecture entirely. Here, the machine does not merely implement commands; it interprets patterns, learns from feedback loops, and adjusts its recommendations accordingly. It does not just automate tasks—it evolves strategies. This evolution alters the conceptual status of the technology. The machine is no longer a conduit for human intent; it is now a co-author of financial direction.

Consider a financial advisor using a CRM integrated with AI-based behavioural analytics. In the automation paradigm, the system might generate alerts—"Client X has not made an ISA contribution this year." In the autonomy paradigm, the system not only flags the missed contribution but also infers that the client's recent expenditure spike may be linked to caregiving duties, predicts that their long-term savings trajectory is at risk, and recommends a new cash-flow strategy based on thousands of similar cases. Crucially, it does this without being told to look for those patterns. The machine moves from task-specific to context-sensitive.

This evolution forces a recalibration of the advisor's role. Historically, the advisor-client relationship was built on asymmetry: the advisor had information, expertise, and access; the client had questions, goals, and uncertainty. Today, AI levels the field in unprecedented ways. Clients equipped with intelligent digital assistants may come to the first meeting already armed with projections, comparisons, and tailored options generated by an app more attentive than any human planner could realistically be. This doesn't eliminate the advisor, but it does demote their role from gatekeeper to interpreter—from financial authority to human validator.

Some argue this represents a threat to the profession. But a closer reading reveals something more nuanced: *a shift from transactional competence to relational intelligence.* Advisors are no longer valued solely for what they know, but for how they help clients *navigate* what the machine knows. In this model, the advisor becomes less of a calculator and more of a counsellor. Less a strategist, more a steward of meaning and judgment in a landscape where information is abundant but understanding is scarce.

The implications run deeper than workflow. AI's autonomy is not simply technical—it is epistemological. It changes how we come to "know" in finance. Traditional models rely on general rules: diversify, save early, avoid unnecessary debt. But AI-based systems generate *individualised probabilities*, not general truths. What is right for one person may not be for another—and the system learns this not through principle, but through experience. A 35-year-old entrepreneur in Singapore may receive a different financial trajectory than a 35-year-old teacher in Scotland, not based on income alone, but on spending psychology, social signals, biometric stress indicators, and location-based behavioural data. The result is a kind of bespoke forecasting previously unimaginable at scale.

Yet with this sophistication comes opacity. The classic critique of machine learning models—particularly deep learning systems—is that they can be functionally correct but philosophically unaccountable. An AI may recommend a high-risk investment strategy based on inferred risk tolerance, but be unable to explain *why* it reached that conclusion in a way that satisfies ethical or fiduciary standards. In finance, where trust is historically grounded in transparency and explanation, this presents a significant challenge.

This opacity does more than frustrate—it reshapes the psychological architecture of trust. Traditionally, trust in an advisor emerged through interpersonal dynamics: responsiveness, empathy, competence. With AI, trust becomes engineered through *interface and output.* Does the platform seem confident? Are the recommendations seamless? Is the dashboard intuitive? These are aesthetic proxies for understanding, and they are easily mistaken for substance. The client may come to trust a system not because it is wise, but because it is *well designed.*

This raises urgent ethical questions. If a client follows AI-generated financial advice and suffers adverse consequences, where does accountability lie? With the firm that deployed the system? The developer who trained it? The user who clicked "Accept"? Unlike human advisors, algorithms cannot be sued, shamed, or retrained in empathy. They do not possess ethics; they merely reflect the ethics of those who build them. Yet in autonomy, the system begins to assume *intentionality* in the eyes of the user. The machine becomes an agent, not just an assistant.

This pseudo-agency is compounded by the increasing ability of AI systems to influence behaviour subtly, even imperceptibly. Through A/B-tested nudges, reinforcement learning loops, and emotion-aware interfaces, AI can guide clients toward actions they might not have otherwise chosen. Whether this is interpreted as empowerment or manipulation depends on the values embedded in the system—and the literacy of the user to detect them. In either case, the advisor must now account not only for the client's intentions, but also for the machine's.

This is where the true redefinition of the advisor-client relationship occurs—not in the elimination of the advisor, but in the multiplication of interlocutors. The conversation is no longer between two human beings. It is triangulated: client, advisor, algorithm. Each brings different knowledge, different biases, and different methods of reasoning. The advisor must now translate not only financial concepts, but *machine logic*—explaining, interpreting, and sometimes challenging outputs that appear objective but are in fact deeply contingent.

This new configuration also complicates consent. A client who receives AI-generated recommendations may believe they are making an informed decision, but in many cases, they are responding to a curated set of options shaped by unseen variables: algorithmic assumptions, economic incentives, platform design. What does informed consent mean when the very framework of choice has been pre-structured by a learning system? And who bears responsibility for ensuring that structure is ethical, intelligible, and aligned with the client's best interests?

None of this is to suggest that AI-driven autonomy is inherently dangerous. On the contrary, the potential benefits are extraordinary. It can democratise access to high-quality advice, reduce human error, personalise planning at scale, and free advisors from administrative tasks to focus on deeper human engagements. But the leap from automation to autonomy demands a new intellectual infrastructure—one that reconsiders not only the tools we use, but the *relationships* those tools produce.

We must ask, for example, what kind of *epistemic humility* advisors will need in a world where machines may outperform them on most quantitative tasks. How do professionals maintain relevance when their knowledge is eclipsed by systems that learn faster and forget less? The answer lies not in resisting the shift, but in *reframing the role*—from information provider to wisdom curator, from planner to partner, from certainty-maker to ambiguity-navigator.

This reframing also requires new forms of education—for advisors and clients alike. Advisors must learn to interrogate algorithms, not just rely on them. They must be able to identify when a system's recommendations, though statistically sound, conflict with a client's values, psychology, or lived experience. Meanwhile, clients must cultivate a basic fluency in how AI systems work—not to master the code, but to question the context.

This is not merely technical adaptation. It is ethical evolution. If financial planning is to remain a human-centred endeavour in the age of intelligent machines, then we must design relationships—not just systems—that prioritise understanding, transparency, and shared authorship. The machine may be autonomous, but the outcomes must still be mutual.

In the end, the shift from automation to autonomy is not about replacing the human advisor. It is about redefining what human expertise looks like in a world where thinking is no longer uniquely ours. The future of financial planning will be shaped not by who has the best algorithm, but by who asks the better questions—about values, about meaning, and about what we ultimately want wealth to serve. That is not a task for machines. That is a responsibility that remains, enduringly, ours.

The Disappearing Middleman

The financial middleman once sat at the centre of the modern economic system. Advisor, broker, banker, underwriter, portfolio manager—titles varied, but the premise remained the same: access to markets, information, and expertise flowed through intermediaries. If you wanted to buy international equities, secure a mortgage, or hedge against currency risk, you needed someone on the inside—someone with credentials, tools, and time. That person wasn't just a facilitator. They were a gatekeeper, a translator, a necessary layer between individual ambition and institutional power. But today, that layer is thinning. Artificial intelligence is rendering many middlemen optional, and some entirely obsolete.

At the core of this change is not simply digital convenience but cognitive compression. AI doesn't just connect clients to data—it collapses the distance between individual users and the historically complex apparatus of global finance. What once required hours of human analysis, institutional clearance, and bespoke portfolio construction can now be replicated by an app trained on thousands of market conditions and behavioural signals. It is no longer science fiction to say that a 23-year-old in Lagos with a smartphone can access financial modelling capabilities that would have been exclusive to Wall Street quants a decade ago. The tools have not just become more powerful—they have become more *available.*

This accessibility is not accidental. It is the result of a strategic convergence between cloud computing, open-source financial data, and increasingly sophisticated machine learning models. Products like Robinhood, eToro, and Wealthfront have helped normalise the idea that algorithmic investing is not just for the ultra-wealthy. But what is most striking is the quiet encroachment of ambient AI into traditionally human-only domains. Chat-based financial assistants now offer retirement planning advice. AI-driven apps forecast tax obligations and automatically allocate funds to optimise post-tax returns. Large language models fine-tuned on economic literature generate investment memos in seconds. For the average user, this does not feel like a revolution. It feels like a set of intuitive upgrades. But under the surface, the architecture of authority is being rewritten.

What does it mean when you no longer need an intermediary to access financial wisdom? The answer is both liberating and disorienting. On one hand, AI democratises financial power. Retail investors can now replicate hedge-fund strategies, backtest investment theses, and receive personalised credit recommendations—all without institutional dependence. The spread of AI-augmented tools represents a long-overdue rebalancing in an industry historically marked by opacity and exclusion. But on the other hand, it removes friction that once acted as a pause for reflection. When middlemen disappear, so too can moments of human inquiry. You don't call your broker. You swipe right. You don't consult a planner. You accept the algorithm's suggestion. Ease and access grow—but so too does abstraction.

This abstraction has material consequences. Consider the case of algorithmic trading apps that encourage fractional investment in trending assets based on short-term momentum. What was once the province of day traders is now gamified for the masses, complete with badges, push notifications, and social sharing. Users feel informed—but are often responding to cues engineered for engagement, not prudence. The middleman once offered a buffer—a human being who could say, "This may not be right for you." In many AI-powered platforms, that voice is gone. Replaced, at best, by risk disclaimers and optional deep-dives that few users read.

This is not to romanticise the legacy financial intermediary. Many were exclusionary, self-interested, and structurally incentivised to preserve their own complexity. But they were human. They could be questioned, held accountable, and—crucially—could account for context. An advisor might counsel a conservative investment not because the spreadsheet said so, but because they knew the client's emotional bandwidth was stretched thin. An underwriter might pause a loan approval not because the credit score was insufficient, but because the borrower's circumstances deserved conversation. AI, in its current form, struggles with this kind of nuance. It optimises based on general patterns, not singular lives.

There is also a deeper epistemological shift at play: the decentralisation of financial authority. Expertise used to reside in recognised institutions—banks, rating agencies, licensed professionals. Now, expertise is embedded in platforms. The interface becomes the advisor. The recommendation engine becomes the strategy. This is empowering, but it also creates new vulnerabilities. If a human advisor misleads you, you can hold them liable. If an algorithm nudges you into poor outcomes based on flawed training data, who do you blame? The app? The developer? The data source?

Regulatory frameworks are only beginning to grapple with these questions. In most jurisdictions, consumer protections still rely on models of agency and liability designed for human actors. A financial advisor has a fiduciary duty. An app has terms and conditions. The disappearance of the middleman not only alters the transaction—it alters the very basis of trust, consent, and accountability. And this becomes especially complex when the AI does not just *execute* financial decisions but *learns* from them, adapting its future recommendations in a feedback loop that the user neither sees nor understands.

One cannot overstate the importance of explainability in this new paradigm. When a traditional advisor recommends a course of action, they are expected to justify it. Even if their reasoning is flawed, it is visible. By contrast, many AI systems operate as black boxes. Their recommendations are often presented with a veneer of confidence, but little intelligibility. Users may receive a suggested asset allocation, a loan offer, or a tax-saving plan without ever understanding the assumptions, trade-offs, or ethical boundaries encoded in the system. And because the experience is seamless, few pause to ask.

This raises the stakes for financial literacy—not in the conventional sense of understanding compound interest or credit utilisation, but in a more conceptual sense: *how to interrogate a system.* How to discern when AI is serving your best interests versus when it is reinforcing platform incentives or historical biases. The disappearance of the middleman demands a new kind of vigilance—one that doesn't resist automation, but critically engages with it.

Yet there is another side to this shift—one that speaks to equity and access. In many parts of the world, the financial middleman never existed at all. In rural India, sub-Saharan Africa, or marginalised communities in the West, professional financial advice has long been an unaffordable luxury. AI offers an unprecedented opportunity to extend financial tools to the historically excluded. Start-ups in Kenya are using AI to assess informal income patterns for micro-lending. In Brazil, robo-advisors are helping gig workers build investment portfolios with no minimum deposit. These are not novelties—they are paradigm shifts. They show what is possible when the distance between person and platform is reduced to a few taps.

Still, access without understanding is not empowerment. And this is the tension that defines the disappearing middleman. The old gatekeepers are falling, but new dependencies are emerging—on data quality, algorithmic fairness, platform design, and the hidden incentives of tech-enabled finance. The burden of discernment has shifted from the institution to the individual. And yet the individual now faces systems that are more opaque, more complex, and more persuasive than anything that preceded them.

To navigate this world requires not a rejection of AI, but a redefinition of trust. Not trust in the human intermediary, but in the design of the system itself. This places enormous responsibility on those building the platforms that replace the middlemen. They are no longer just product designers. They are *architects of financial cognition*—deciding how users see, decide, and act. Every toggle, every notification, every risk visualisation is a subtle form of governance.

And so the question is no longer: will AI eliminate the middleman? That process is well underway. The real question is: what kind of financial relationship emerges in its absence? One that is shallow and frictionless, or one that is transparent, informed, and dignifying? One that replicates old exclusions in digital form, or one that genuinely redistributes power? The disappearance of the middleman is not the end of mediation—it is the beginning of a new, machine-augmented form of it. Whether that form respects the complexity of human lives is not a technological question. It is an ethical one. And it remains, fundamentally, ours to answer.

The Rise of Invisible Planning

At some point, many people stopped budgeting. Not because they mastered it, but because their phones started doing it for them. Savings were quietly siphoned off into digital envelopes. Bills were anticipated and paid without notice. Investment contributions occurred regularly, but few could explain exactly when or why. What began as convenience is now becoming default: finance that runs itself. This is not automation in the classic sense of task execution—it is ambient financial intelligence, embedded seamlessly into daily life, operating in the background without friction, and often without deliberate input. Welcome to the age of invisible planning.

Ambient finance refers to the integration of AI-driven financial functions into everyday technologies, functioning subtly, intuitively, and persistently. It's the budgeting app that rounds up your spare change and funnels it into a diversified ETF. It's the salary-splitting system that directs income into separate pots for rent, discretionary spending, and long-term savings—based not on fixed percentages but adaptive algorithms learning from your transaction patterns. It's the predictive software that sees a dip in your energy usage and adjusts your utility payment schedule, or the AI assistant that suggests deferring a discretionary purchase based on upcoming expenses it detected in your calendar. The user is still nominally "in control," but control itself is being reframed. The essence of planning—once a conscious, cognitive activity—is now diffused into processes we do not always see or remember authorising.

This invisibility is not accidental. It is a design strategy, often lauded as frictionless UX. The ideal is to remove barriers to action, eliminate complexity, and spare users from decision fatigue. The underlying assumption is persuasive: people don't plan well on their own, so we should build systems that do it for them, quietly and efficiently. And in many cases, it works. Savings rates rise when contributions are automated. Late fees drop when payments are pre-scheduled. Behavioural nudges embedded into user interfaces reduce impulsive purchases and encourage healthier habits. But the question is no longer whether ambient finance *works*—it is *what kind of agency it produces*, and *at what cost.*

There is a critical difference between *ease* and *understanding.* A system that successfully diverts 10% of your monthly income into an investment account may be helping you—but if you don't know that it's happening, or why, the relationship between you and your financial future becomes mediated by a form of intelligence that operates beyond your attention. What does it mean to be a financially responsible person in such a system? Is it enough to configure the settings once and let the software optimise in perpetuity? Or is responsibility something that must be exercised, periodically, through reflection and adjustment?

One of the unspoken consequences of invisible planning is the erosion of *experiential feedback.* In traditional financial behaviour, cause and effect are linked. You spend too much; your account depletes. You save deliberately; you feel the reward. In ambient finance, these connections are abstracted. You might receive a push notification that your "Safeguard Fund" has increased by £50, but this gain was not the result of a deliberate action—it was a background process triggered by algorithms. Financial behaviour becomes something observed, not enacted. And this has implications for how we internalise goals, discipline, and achievement.

The broader question here is philosophical: what role does *conscious effort* play in the moral architecture of personal finance? In cultures that prize self-discipline and intentionality—where saving is a virtue and planning a skill—ambient finance challenges deep-seated norms. If a machine can do it better, faster, and with less stress, why insist on personal involvement? The answer lies not in romanticising struggle but in recognising the relational and reflective dimensions of planning. Financial decisions are rarely about numbers alone.

They are about values, trade-offs, aspirations, and fears. A system that optimises your cash flow but bypasses your capacity for introspection may be efficient—but it risks rendering the financial self less articulate, less engaged, and ultimately, less sovereign.

This introduces a key tension: between *assistance* and *substitution*. When does helpfulness become paternalism? When does delegation become disempowerment? In most ambient financial systems today, the user retains a nominal veto power. Settings can be changed, preferences adjusted, accounts disconnected. But the interface design often discourages interference. Defaults are sticky. Customisation is buried behind friction. Notifications are designed to reassure, not provoke inquiry. The system whispers: "We've got this covered." And for most users, that's enough—until it's not.

Consider the example of an AI-enhanced savings app used by a young freelancer. It analyses her income and spending history, detects volatility in cash flow, and adjusts her savings schedule dynamically to avoid overdrafts. In doing so, it prevents financial stress and builds long-term security. But over time, she loses track of how much is being saved, when, and for what. When an unexpected medical bill arrives, she is surprised to learn that her liquidity is lower than assumed. The system had optimised for regularity, not flexibility. The ambient nature of the planning created a sense of safety, but not an accurate awareness of the underlying trade-offs.

This is not an edge case. It reflects a structural challenge in the design of ambient finance: how to preserve *cognitive accountability* in systems that aim to remove cognitive load. Transparency alone is not sufficient. Users don't read data logs. They don't audit settings regularly. What's needed is a reimagining of *financial dialogue*—not between two humans, but between human and machine. Interfaces must evolve from dashboards to conversations, from transactional nudges to narrative explanations. The system should not only act but explain *why* it acts—and invite the user to confirm, question, or redirect that action in a meaningful way.

There are emerging models attempting to do just that. Some platforms now incorporate "explainable AI" frameworks into financial recommendations, offering plain-language rationales for adjustments. Others allow users to simulate different behavioural profiles—"What if I spent like I did six months ago?"—to see how their financial trajectory would shift. But these features are still rare and often treated as advanced options rather than core design elements. The dominant ethos remains one of efficiency through invisibility.

Yet invisibility has limits, particularly in matters involving consent. Passive agreement—clicking "I agree" once during setup—should not be mistaken for enduring, informed participation. Consent in ambient finance must be *continual*, *context-sensitive*, and *revocable*. Systems must anticipate not only financial trends but shifts in user intent and comprehension. A 25-year-old saving for a holiday has different priorities than a 35-year-old preparing for parenthood or a 55-year-old managing health risks. A system that does not recognise these life inflection points risks optimising for a version of the user that no longer exists.

Moreover, ambient finance operates in a cultural context where financial literacy is unevenly distributed. The very people who might benefit most from seamless planning—those underbanked, financially anxious, or overwhelmed by cognitive load—are also the most at risk of surrendering too much agency. If invisible systems are trusted blindly, they may become opaque custodians of someone's economic future, encoding assumptions and biases without the user's knowledge or ability to challenge them.

This brings us to the heart of the matter: *what kind of financial autonomy do we want to preserve in the age of ambient intelligence?* Autonomy does not require total control, but it does require *awareness* and *meaningful choice.* It demands that systems inform, not infantilise. That they support human decision-making without subsuming it. That they enable participation, not passive compliance.

To achieve this, the next generation of ambient finance must centre *relational design*. This means designing not just for outcomes, but for experiences of agency. It involves embedding moments of reflective pause—digital prompts that ask users if their goals have changed, if they wish to reprioritise, or if they understand the consequences of current settings. It also means creating space for financial storytelling: tools that let users articulate, track, and evolve their financial narratives alongside the numbers.

Invisible planning is not inherently problematic. In many cases, it protects users from volatility, impulsiveness, and fatigue. It cushions the sharp edges of modern financial life. But if it becomes the dominant mode of engagement, it risks hollowing out the very capacity that financial planning is meant to nurture: the ability to think about the future in a way that is reflective, values-driven, and self-authored.

The challenge, then, is to design for *invisible scaffolding*, not invisible substitution. Let the system carry weight—but let the human still see the architecture. Let the system advise—but keep the individual awake. Because the goal of planning has never been just to optimise money. It has always been to clarify life. And no system—however intelligent—can do that without us.

What Money Can't See

There is a deeply held assumption in modern finance—and increasingly in the design of AI-driven financial systems—that more data leads to better decisions. That the complexity of human lives, if only measured finely enough, can be translated into optimal financial outcomes. From biometrics to spending histories, from social graphs to geolocation trails, the digital fingerprints we leave behind are being harvested to tell a story: a story of risk, desire, reliability, and potential. Algorithms parse it. Dashboards visualise it. And we are told: this is who you are, this is what you need, this is the best choice for your future. But there is a fundamental problem. *No amount of data, however precise, can fully capture the weight of human context.*

The idea that financial decisions can be improved by increasing their informational basis is not inherently flawed. At the level of efficiency—minimising fees, maximising tax advantages, identifying patterns of wasteful spending—data has indeed been transformative. Machine learning models now outperform traditional underwriters in credit risk scoring. Portfolio management algorithms can rebalance with uncanny precision. Even household budgeting tools can alert users to patterns they would never have noticed unaided. But what these systems offer in optimisation, they often lack in interpretation. They see transactions, not intentions. Correlation, not meaning.

This becomes clear when we examine how AI systems attempt to model human life. A person with inconsistent income, several short-term loans, and no formal employment may be flagged as high-risk. The data suggests instability. But the algorithm does not see that this person is a caregiver juggling multiple informal jobs while supporting dependents. It does not know the community reliance placed on her generosity, or the cultural expectations behind her financial choices. It cannot model the psychological calculus of dignity, shame, sacrifice, or resilience. These are not statistical anomalies—they are the normative texture of life for billions of people. And *they resist quantification by design.*

This limitation is not just a technical gap; it is a conceptual blind spot. It reflects a broader belief that financial behaviour can be understood purely in terms of numbers—how much we save, how often we spend, how predictably we pay. But people are not spreadsheets. They are situated beings with histories, traumas, hopes, and contradictions. Financial decisions are rarely reducible to economic logic alone. They are entangled with memory, morality, and emotion. A person may reject a perfectly rational refinancing offer not because it's financially unsound, but because it came from a company they perceive as exploitative. Another may keep paying off a relative's debts, against all advice, because family honour trumps individual solvency.

These motivations are not irrational—they are *non-quantifiable.* And this is where AI's promise meets its boundary. Machine learning thrives on what is measurable. It needs input/output relationships, structured features, labelled outcomes. But some of the most important variables in financial life—trust, regret, loyalty, identity—cannot be easily encoded. Nor should they be. Attempts to force these dimensions into quantifiable proxies risk distorting rather than revealing the truth. Sentiment analysis might infer anxiety from a client's typing speed or word choice, but it cannot understand the nuance of a financial trauma triggered by an innocuous email. A credit model may incorporate non-traditional indicators like mobile phone usage or social network activity, but it still cannot see the informal economies and survival strategies that define life outside the formal sector.

This is not merely an ethical concern. It is a design problem. When we assume that better data leads to better decisions, we risk overfitting models to the world as it has been measured—often by those in positions of privilege—and underfitting them to the world as it is *lived* by those on the margins. The danger is not just exclusion; it is misrepresentation. AI may confidently assign a risk score, but the confidence does not guarantee accuracy—only consistency with the model's internal logic. And when these scores are used to make decisions about lending, insurance, employment, or investment, the human cost of misrecognition can be profound.

One might argue that all systems are reductive—that even human advisors rely on mental shortcuts and biases. This is true, but with a crucial distinction: *humans can be challenged.* A client can push back against an advisor's assumptions, explain their reasoning, appeal to shared values. There is room for conversation, negotiation, reflection. With an algorithm, the verdict often arrives without explanation. Worse, it may arrive *without awareness.* Invisible algorithms shape loan approvals, limit credit card offers, tailor financial recommendations—all without explicit user engagement. The decisions feel ambient, neutral, objective. But they are, in fact, the outputs of highly contingent models trained on partial realities.

This raises the question of *financial dignity*. What does it mean to be seen—truly seen—by a system designed to assist you? Does it mean being correctly classified? Efficiently managed? Or does it mean being treated as someone whose life cannot be fully understood through metrics? There is a difference between a system that predicts your behaviour and one that respects your complexity. The former optimises for outcomes. The latter creates space for agency, anomaly, and change.

It also raises the question of *who decides what matters*. In any modelling process, choices are made: which variables to include, which outcomes to prioritise, which historical patterns to replicate. These are not neutral decisions. They reflect the values of designers, institutions, and data providers. A fintech company that prioritises short-term return may recommend aggressive investing strategies to clients whose personalities are risk-averse. An AI budgeting app may penalise users for spending on what it deems "non-essential," without understanding that a weekly visit to a parent is not a luxury, but an act of care. When systems decide what counts, they also shape what is considered *responsible behaviour*.

This shaping power is subtle but profound. It turns platforms into pedagogies—users learn what is "good" or "bad" behaviour based on what the system rewards or penalises. Over time, this can standardise financial life in ways that stifle diversity. Cultural practices around saving, gifting, borrowing, or debt may be labelled inefficient or irrational by models trained on Western financial norms. Users may begin to conform, not because they believe the model is right, but because the model has become the metric for legitimacy. *The cost of being misaligned is exclusion*—from access, from offers, from opportunities.

So what does it mean to design financial intelligence systems that acknowledge the limits of what money can see? It begins with humility. Designers, developers, and financial institutions must recognise that no model captures the whole of a person's life. They must resist the temptation to treat every deviation from the model as error rather than expression. And they must build systems that not only explain their recommendations, but invite users to contest, contextualise, or override them.

It also requires pluralism. Financial AI should not aspire to a single universal model of behaviour, but should accommodate multiple understandings of value, time, risk, and obligation. A planner in Tokyo may prioritise long-term stability over short-term gain; a worker in Nairobi may see remittances as more central than personal wealth accumulation. Systems should reflect these differences, not erase them. This means building modular, adaptive frameworks—not just intelligent, but *interpretable* and *responsive* to human meaning.

Ultimately, the assumption that more data leads to better financial decisions overlooks a more foundational truth: that wisdom is not the same as information, and judgment is not the same as prediction. The most meaningful financial choices often require us to act against the model, to choose uncertainty over optimisation, to invest in people rather than portfolios, to value presence over profit. No amount of data can see those decisions in full. But we can—and we must—design financial systems that leave room for what data cannot see. That is not a limitation. It is a sign of respect for the irreducible richness of human life.

Chapter 2
Reprogramming Desire

Desire has always been the quiet motor of finance. Strip away the charts, the risk models, the actuarial tables, and what you find beneath is longing—sometimes raw, sometimes refined. It is the hope of freedom, the fear of insufficiency, the wish to be admired, the need to feel safe, the urge to leave a trace behind. Money itself is seldom the goal. It is the symbol, the stand-in, for what we imagine it will buy us. That much has never changed. What is changing—swiftly, subtly, almost imperceptibly—is how those desires are shaped.

The old framework of financial identity—whether you considered yourself a saver, spender, investor, or perhaps a reluctant avoider—was largely a product of upbringing and circumstance. A childhood in a household marked by scarcity might wire someone towards caution and conservation. A childhood in a family of entrepreneurs could produce an appetite for risk, speculation as a form of self-expression. These patterns were sticky, but not permanent. They shifted slowly, through habit, failure, and the passing of time. Today, however, that gradual evolution is being compressed, accelerated, and, increasingly, engineered.

Your "financial self" is no longer simply a by-product of experience and culture. It has become a dataset—observed, profiled, adjusted in real time by intelligent systems that do not merely respond to preference but actively mould it. Every transaction, every search query, every lingering second on a financial page feeds into models that predict, recommend, and nudge. This is more than personalisation; it is behavioural authorship, a form of scripting that reshapes identity at its roots.

Fintech platforms already deploy behavioural analytics to build and refine user archetypes. A cautious depositor who shuns risk is quickly tagged as conservative. Another, flitting between speculative crypto bets and consumer debt, is slotted as opportunistic. These aren't idle classifications. They dictate which products are displayed, how interfaces are designed, even the tone in which "advice" is offered. But therein lies the paradox: the more you engage, the more your future self is tethered to your past behaviour. Systems optimised to anticipate who you already appear to be can narrow the possibility of becoming someone else.

The dynamic shifts again when we look at how AI cultivates desire itself. Once, aspiration was a slow brew of culture, advertising, and peer influence. Now it is micro-targeted. Tailored. Engineered. A millennial with a penchant for sustainable travel and ethical fashion may find investment products pitched as "climate-smart journeys." A Gen Z freelancer with volatile income might be lured into fractional shares of Tesla, not sold as an investment but as a cultural badge. These are not accidental strategies. They are deliberate, algorithmic interventions—tested, refined, optimised—crafted to hook into the intersection of identity, emotion, and longing.

Designers of these platforms experiment relentlessly. Interest rates are A/B tested alongside metaphors. Colour schemes are fine-tuned to encourage deposits. The timing of notifications is tweaked until it aligns with your personal dopamine cycle. In such an environment, financial tools do not merely accompany your goals. They influence them, and that influence is rarely visible.

Naturally, ethical questions rise. When does guidance cross into manipulation? When does personalisation begin to look like surveillance? Gamification adds another layer. Apps hand out badges for saving streaks, flash celebratory animations when investments are made, rank users on community leaderboards. For some, these mechanisms encourage discipline. For others, they trigger compulsive behaviour, the same neural circuits exploited by casinos and social media platforms firing again in the name of "engagement."

Defenders argue that gamification lowers barriers, making finance approachable for people otherwise alienated from it. There is merit in this. Yet not all attention is equal, and not all engagement is benign. An app that cheers every trade risks fostering reckless overactivity. A savings tool that incessantly nudges users to "do more" might compound the psychological toll of precarious living.

What begins as empowerment can curdle into anxiety disguised as agency.

Beneath it all lies the central fact: attention itself has become the commodity. In an AI-driven financial ecosystem, the longer you stay, the more the system learns, and the richer the predictions it can monetise. Financial platforms are no longer just part of the economy; they are embedded in the attention economy, competing with social media and streaming services for your focus. Your time, your clicks, your hesitation—all are currency, all converted into data, all recycled into profit.

This convergence alters the very rhythm of financial planning. What was once periodic—annual reviews, quarterly check-ins—now becomes continuous. A thousand micro-interactions, each nudged, logged, and folded into the next. The distinctions between consumption and investment, between leisure and planning, blur. When an investment prompt appears beside a playlist suggestion or a dating notification, the category of "finance" itself begins to dissolve. Money becomes one more theatre of attention.

And here, a harder question: whose desires are these? If a machine learns what you want before you consciously articulate it, if it adjusts your aims based on probabilities rather than declared intentions, who exactly is doing the wanting? The question goes to the marrow of autonomy. If choices are the product of unseen influences, filtered through algorithms you neither understand nor notice, then what remains of agency?

This chapter turns toward these questions. First, the psychology of financial identity in the feedback loops of AI: how the archetypes of spender, saver, investor are reinforced—or rewritten—by machine observation. Then, the mechanics of micro-targeted aspiration: how technology reframes not just what we buy or save for, but what we are taught to want. From there, the ethics of gamification: when design becomes coercion. Finally, the monetisation of attention itself, and what it means when finance is no longer about numbers alone but about the capture of consciousness.

The claim here is not that AI corrupts desire. It reshapes it—renders it pliable, measurable, commodifiable. That can mean better advice, timelier nudges, broader participation. But the power to sculpt desire is never neutral. It is a responsibility of the highest order. As machines assume more of this role, the urgent task is to interrogate not only what we want, but what kind of selves we become in learning to want within systems designed to anticipate us.

Finance has always looked to the future. But in this new landscape, it is also about the future of wanting itself. To understand it, we must look hard at the tools shaping our longings, the identities we adopt, and the choices we claim as our own. The most profound impact of AI on finance may not be how it manages our money at all—but how it teaches us to desire.

The Psychology of Financial Identity

Ask someone to describe their relationship with money, and you are unlikely to receive a strictly financial response. Instead, you'll hear a story—shaped by childhood memories, cultural messages, emotional triggers, and personal beliefs. Some will say, "I've always been terrible with money," or "I'm a natural saver," or "Investing just isn't for me." These are not neutral observations; they are expressions of identity. Beneath the spreadsheets and budgeting apps, most financial behaviour is driven not by logic, but by *self-perception.* We act, not as calculators, but as characters in a narrative we believe to be true about who we are when it comes to money.

Financial identity refers to the internalised roles we adopt—consciously or otherwise—about how we engage with financial decisions. These roles are patterned: saver, spender, investor, hoarder, denier, planner, avoider. They are influenced by upbringing, cultural norms, past experiences, and feedback from others. A child who grows up hearing that "money doesn't grow on trees" may form a scarcity-driven identity, deeply cautious with spending. Another, raised in an environment where financial literacy was actively taught and modelled, may adopt the role of confident planner or risk-tolerant investor. These identities become lenses through which people interpret financial information, make choices, and even judge others.

What makes financial identity especially sticky is the role of feedback loops. Behaviour shapes identity, which then reinforces behaviour. A person who impulsively spends during periods of stress may begin to view themselves as "bad with money," leading to further avoidance, guilt, and loss of control. Conversely, someone who sees early success with saving may internalise the identity of a disciplined saver, even if that pattern was circumstantial rather than intrinsic. Over time, these identities harden, becoming part of a person's psychological operating system—often outside of conscious awareness.

Historically, these feedback loops were primarily social and experiential. You learned about money through trial and error, by observing others, or by interacting with advisors who offered validation or correction. Financial institutions operated with slow feedback cycles: monthly statements, annual reviews, long-term plans. There was space for reflection, for the reinterpretation of past behaviour, for the redefinition of identity. But that landscape is shifting. The rise of AI-driven financial platforms is collapsing these feedback cycles—making them real-time, personalised, and psychologically sticky in ways that are both powerful and potentially limiting.

Today's financial systems are not passive record-keepers. They are *adaptive mirrors*. Apps track your spending, investing, saving, and even browsing patterns. They form models of your preferences and habits, and then reflect those models back to you—through customised recommendations, behavioural nudges, and goal-setting suggestions. These platforms don't just observe your financial identity—they participate in shaping it.

Take, for example, the growing use of categorised spending summaries. If a user is consistently shown that their discretionary spending is "above average," accompanied by cautionary emojis or colour-coded warnings, the implicit message is not merely informative—it is identity-shaping. The user may come to see themselves as undisciplined or excessive, regardless of the context or intent behind the purchases. If, instead, their investments are praised through gamified badges or achievement milestones, a different identity is reinforced: that of the savvy investor, even if the gains are marginal or the risks poorly understood.

AI intensifies these effects by tailoring feedback with high precision. It does not offer generic advice; it offers *you-specific guidance*, inferred from patterns you may not even recognise in yourself. Over time, this creates a loop in which the system not only responds to your financial self but actively conditions it. If you behave like a spender, you are shown products for spenders. If you behave like a saver, you are encouraged to double down on austerity. The algorithm rewards consistency, not necessarily reflection or growth. And this matters, because *identity is shaped not just by what we do, but by what the world reflects back to us.*

There are profound implications here. On one hand, AI has the potential to support positive financial transformation. A person trying to shift from spender to saver can benefit from real-time nudges, personalised savings goals, and visual reinforcement. These tools can scaffold new behaviours and make abstract goals feel tangible. But the very power of this feedback mechanism also introduces risk. If a system reinforces existing behaviours without offering pathways for change, it can trap users in financial identities that no longer serve them. Worse, it may pathologise behaviour without understanding context—treating generosity as recklessness, or risk-aversion as ignorance.

This dynamic is especially concerning in populations already marginalised by traditional financial systems. For example, a young gig worker with fluctuating income may be classified as financially unstable by an AI model trained on salaried patterns. If this identity becomes the basis for product access, credit scoring, or advisory recommendations, the user may be excluded from opportunities or nudged toward suboptimal behaviours—not because of their actual financial capacity, but because of how they have been algorithmically interpreted. The system becomes not a tool for empowerment, but a mechanism of soft exclusion.

The problem is compounded by the invisibility of the modelling process. Most users are unaware of the identity categories being constructed around them. They experience only the interface—the options shown, the defaults suggested, the tone of alerts and reminders. But behind those surfaces are probabilistic models making inferences about their risk tolerance, decision-making style, and psychological triggers. These inferences are often correct in a narrow sense—based on past behaviour—but that correctness can be misleading. Just because a user has avoided investing in the past does not mean they are inherently risk-averse. It may simply mean they were never shown an accessible on-ramp. But if the system interprets them as avoidant, they may never be shown one at all.

The solution is not to abandon adaptive systems, but to interrogate how they frame identity. Financial platforms must recognise that behaviour is not destiny, and that identity is not static. They must design for *identity elasticity*—creating room for users to explore, evolve, and re-author their financial narratives. This could mean giving users greater visibility into how they are being modelled, allowing them to challenge or override classifications. It could mean incorporating prompts for reflection, rather than just feedback—asking why a user chose a particular action, or how they felt about it. It could also mean designing for anomaly—not treating deviation as error, but as signal.

There is also a role for human advisors in this evolving landscape—not as calculators, but as identity mentors. As AI takes over much of the technical planning, human advisors can focus on helping clients interpret their financial lives in context. They can ask the questions machines do not: What does wealth mean to you? What values are you trying to honour? What stories have you inherited about money—and which ones no longer fit? In doing so, they can help clients reclaim authorship over identities that may have been unconsciously shaped by algorithms.

Ultimately, financial identity is not just a descriptor. It is a driver of behaviour, a scaffold of aspiration, and a lens through which we assess success, failure, and possibility. As AI becomes more deeply embedded in the financial lives of individuals, it is not enough to optimise for outcomes. We must also design with an awareness of how these systems affect the way people see themselves—and what they believe they are capable of becoming. Because if we do not challenge the scripts being written around us, we may end up performing roles we never chose, in stories we never meant to tell. And in the realm of finance, where identity shapes action, that performance has real consequences.

Micro-targeted Dreams

Aspirations are not born in isolation. They are shaped—by culture, family, media, and increasingly, by algorithms. We often think of our financial goals as self-authored: I want to buy a house, start a business, retire early. But these desires are now subtly co-produced in real time by digital systems that predict what we might want next and then craft experiences that make that future feel both desirable and achievable. In the age of AI-enhanced financial platforms, aspiration has become a product—packaged, priced, and optimised for conversion. The architecture of dreaming has shifted.

What used to be a matter of delayed gratification and long-term planning is now framed through hyper-personalised prompts delivered through interfaces that study and adapt to our behaviour. Fintech apps and robo-advisors no longer wait for users to declare their goals. They infer them. A few keystrokes, a tap on a preference, or even passively collected behavioural signals are enough to build a predictive profile of who you are and what you're likely to value. That profile then drives the curation of future-facing narratives—investment pathways, savings plans, and financial incentives—designed not only to fulfil your aspirations, but to *construct them.*

Consider the case of the U.S.-based investment platform Stash. Its onboarding process does not begin with asset classes or portfolio theories. Instead, it opens with questions about lifestyle ambitions: "What are you saving for?" "What kind of future do you want?" The user is invited to select from options like "Start a family," "Travel more," or "Be my own boss." These choices are then translated into tailored portfolios framed around aspirational themes—"Clean Energy," "Global Citizen," "Tech Giants." The financial product is not positioned as a rational instrument. It's a vehicle for identity expression. The platform doesn't just manage money—it curates dreams.

A similar dynamic plays out in European platforms like Emma or Plum, where AI-driven spending analysis is used to construct micro-narratives about your lifestyle. "Looks like you eat out often—what if you redirected just £25 per week into your 'Weekend Getaway' fund?" The implication is clear: aspiration is modular. It can be assembled from patterns, nudged into alignment, and then visualised with progress trackers and goal meters that simulate achievement long before the dream materialises. Financial behaviour becomes gamified desire reinforcement.

What's striking is how seamlessly this process bypasses traditional introspection. Where earlier generations might have set goals through deliberate reflection—perhaps during annual financial planning meetings—today's users are often nudged into aspiration through ambient engagement. You didn't know you wanted to retire at 52 until the app suggested it. You hadn't considered investing in ethical robotics until a micro-investment platform presented a neatly packaged thematic fund. The system's ability to anticipate your psychological triggers—risk tolerance, lifestyle envy, social comparison—means that the aspiration appears organically. But the data trails it follows are anything but random.

This raises important questions about authorship. Who is writing the script of financial aspiration in a world where AI can anticipate your next move more accurately than your conscious self? When the system knows you're feeling anxious—because your spending pattern has become erratic—and shows you a calming message about long-term security, is it supporting you or shaping you? When it notices you pause on an image of a beach house, then starts populating your feed with mortgage calculators and retirement models centred on coastal living, is it serving your dream or manufacturing it?

The psychology of this interaction is layered. Research into predictive personalisation suggests that when people receive recommendations that "feel" right—even if they don't know why—they are more likely to trust the system and comply. This compliance, in turn, generates more behavioural data, which tightens the loop of personalisation. The result is a feedback cycle where your desires are continually adjusted to align with what the system thinks you can achieve, what it wants you to want, or what others like you have wanted before. *Aspiration becomes predictive conformity.*

There are benefits to this, of course. Many users find motivation in visualising progress, even if the goal was system-suggested. In behavioural economics, this is referred to as "goal gradient effect"—the tendency to increase effort as one nears a goal. If an app helps a financially overwhelmed user save for their first holiday in years, that is a real and positive outcome. But the ethical tension lies in *directionality*. When systems become so good at anticipating our likely preferences, they may stop offering *alternatives* altogether. The AI doesn't tell you that you could want something radically different—it tells you that, based on people like you, this is probably what you want. The future is narrowed, not expanded.

Contrast this with the human financial advisor of old. A thoughtful advisor might have asked, "Why is this important to you?" or "What would this mean for your family?" or "Are you sure this goal aligns with your values?" These questions weren't efficient, but they were expansive. They created room for contradiction, doubt, and growth. They respected the fluidity of human aspiration. By contrast, the AI's job is not to explore ambiguity—it is to resolve it, statistically. The best-performing platforms are those that can *predict desire quickly and act on it decisively*. Subtle uncertainty, philosophical tension, or long-term evolution are not rewarded in that model.

This design logic—efficiency over ambiguity—also ties aspiration to monetisation. In many fintech platforms, user engagement with goal-setting features directly correlates with conversion to paid products. Robo-advisors often offer tiered services, where setting more complex goals unlocks new tools, investment opportunities, or insurance offers. This isn't inherently problematic—after all, businesses need revenue—but it complicates the trust equation. If the platform benefits from nudging you toward a particular goal, can its recommendations be treated as neutral? When aspiration is a monetisable asset, its authenticity becomes harder to assess.

The same dynamic is now expanding into embedded finance—where financial services are seamlessly integrated into non-financial platforms. Ride-share drivers are prompted to save for vehicle upgrades mid-shift. Creators on content platforms are offered AI-generated investment paths based on anticipated ad revenue. Even lifestyle apps—fitness, wellness, dating—are integrating micro-investing features aligned with user behaviour. These platforms are not traditional financial services; they are attention infrastructures. And they are beginning to shape dreams based not on long-term planning principles, but on behavioural engagement metrics.

This convergence of commerce, psychology, and data science makes financial aspiration more responsive than ever before—but also more susceptible to capture. If your goals can be adjusted in real time to maximise your retention or average revenue per user, then they are no longer simply *yours*. They are co-authored by incentives you don't see and systems you don't control.

That does not mean AI-driven aspiration is inherently dangerous. On the contrary, it can provide access, scaffolding, and visibility to people who have historically been excluded from traditional planning tools. It can surface dormant goals, reduce inertia, and give form to futures that once felt inaccessible. But it demands transparency, literacy, and—perhaps most importantly—*deliberation*. We must create space, in both technology and culture, for people to ask: Do I truly want this, or am I being trained to want it?

This is where the role of design becomes critical. Fintech platforms must resist the urge to flatten desire into behavioural archetypes. They must build systems that *support reflection*, not just prediction. This might include features that show users what goals others in their demographic typically choose—but also those they typically don't. It could mean allowing users to write open-ended aspirations, even if they defy categorisation. It could involve narrative prompts that ask users to revisit goals over time and evaluate whether they still resonate. These are not technically complex features. They are culturally and philosophically motivated design choices. They shift the platform's purpose from aspiration delivery to aspiration discovery.

Aspiration is not a market segment. It is a human impulse—messy, mutable, and often irrational. In the age of micro-targeted dreams, we must be vigilant about whose interests are served by making dreams so measurable. The goal is not to discard predictive tools, but to ensure they are used in service of freedom, not conformity. Because the power to predict what someone wants is also the power to *shape who they become.* And that power, if left unexamined, will not merely change the way we plan. It will rewrite the future we think is ours.

Addiction or Empowerment?

A brightly coloured badge appears on your phone screen: *"Streak Unbroken! You've saved for 7 days straight."* A green progress bar inches forward as you set aside another £10 into your "Dream Holiday" pot. The app offers a friendly high-five emoji, and just below, a message: *"You're in the top 10% of savers like you this week."* What appears, on the surface, to be a moment of financial motivation is something more complex: a behavioural nudge engineered through gamification. The question is no longer whether these nudges work—they do. The question is whether they work in ways that empower individuals, or whether they nudge so effectively that they start to encroach upon autonomy.

Gamification in finance is now ubiquitous. From banking apps to investment platforms, elements of game design—progress tracking, goal visualisation, tiered rewards, social comparison—have been adopted to drive engagement. Proponents argue that these mechanisms foster discipline, break through inertia, and make financial tasks more approachable. For users who find budgeting tedious or saving abstract, a dose of digital encouragement can mean the difference between disengagement and meaningful action. But this line of reasoning overlooks a crucial reality: *engagement is not the same as empowerment*, and motivation does not always align with wellbeing.

The core principle behind gamification is borrowed from behavioural economics: humans are more likely to follow through on goals when they are presented in manageable steps, coupled with instant feedback. But in AI-driven systems, this logic becomes supercharged. Algorithms continuously learn what keeps users active and optimise the reward structure accordingly. What begins as a gentle prompt can quickly evolve into a sophisticated feedback loop, customised for psychological sensitivity and reinforced through real-time analytics. As a result, the line between motivation and manipulation is not only thin—it is dynamic and invisible.

This ambiguity is particularly sharp in fintech products designed to promote habits like micro-saving and retail investing. Consider the app *Acorns*, which rounds up spare change from everyday purchases and invests the difference. Its interface celebrates even the smallest contributions, offering congratulatory animations and subtle social proof: "Join 10 million others growing their future." Similarly, the UK-based app *Moneybox* invites users to set weekly savings challenges and displays encouraging graphics when targets are met. These cues are effective in establishing behavioural momentum. But they also make use of psychological levers typically associated with gambling and compulsive gaming: intermittent reinforcement, escalation, comparison.

When these mechanisms are paired with AI, the ethical complexity intensifies. Machine learning models are trained to identify friction points where users drop off—and to experiment with interface tweaks that reduce those moments of resistance. If a user hesitates to invest in a volatile asset, the app may suggest a lower-risk version with the same theme. If a user fails to meet a goal one week, the streak feature may be temporarily hidden to preserve morale. These changes are subtle but powerful, and they are rarely transparent. The user feels supported, but the system is primarily optimised for retention.

This creates a tension at the heart of AI-driven financial design: *the user's best interest versus the platform's business model.* Most fintech apps are freemium or transaction-based, meaning revenue depends on continued usage and behavioural compliance. That compliance may align with long-term financial health—but it may not. A platform that encourages users to save aggressively without accounting for their need for short-term liquidity could inadvertently cause harm. Similarly, encouraging novice users to "level up" into more complex investment products may generate fees but introduce risk well beyond the user's comprehension.

Designing for empowerment means more than encouraging positive habits. It requires *respecting context.* An AI system may correctly infer that a user is motivated by competition and therefore show them a savings leaderboard. But what if that comparison triggers anxiety, or reinforces feelings of inadequacy for users with erratic income or financial trauma? Is the system tracking the emotional effect of its nudges—or just the click-through rate? Without mechanisms to audit emotional impact, gamified interfaces risk prioritising short-term behavioural outcomes over psychological resilience.

It is also worth noting how deeply cultural values shape our interpretation of gamified finance. In the West, gamification is often framed as a form of individual empowerment: make finance fun, turn planning into a challenge, reward discipline. But in collectivist cultures, where financial decision-making is more interdependent, this framing may appear trivialising or even alienating. The gamified "win" of reaching a solo retirement goal may feel empty to users whose priorities are family care, community contribution, or religious obligations that don't translate easily into goal metrics. Designing universally effective nudges without accounting for these value systems is both a technical and ethical failure.

Another underexplored dimension is *cognitive availability.* Gamification often relies on users interacting frequently with an app—checking in, responding to prompts, updating goals. But not all users have the same cognitive bandwidth. A single parent managing multiple jobs may lack the energy to optimise their budget every evening. A user with ADHD may struggle to maintain consistent engagement, especially if the app's design rewards streaks and penalises missed days. If empowerment requires regular interaction, and interaction is unequally distributed, then the empowerment is unequally delivered.

This raises a broader philosophical point: *should effective financial systems demand our attention, or preserve it?* Gamified apps, by design, are attention-seeking. They thrive on notifications, feedback, and visual cues. But there is an alternative model: tools that aim to remove cognitive burden rather than attract it—designed not to engage, but to support invisibly. This doesn't preclude gamification, but it reframes its purpose. Instead of motivating users to "check in," the system could quietly optimise in the background, surfacing only when meaningful input is needed. Empowerment, in this model, is measured not by frequency of use but by depth of understanding and alignment with life context.

The ethical test for AI-driven gamification is not whether it increases savings rates or trading volumes. It is whether it does so *in a way that reinforces dignity, transparency, and genuine autonomy*. That means exposing the logic of the nudge—why this goal, why now, who benefits? It means offering opt-outs not just for features, but for entire behavioural models. And it means conducting ongoing assessment not only of performance metrics, but of emotional outcomes: does the system leave users feeling more in control, more informed, more capable—or merely more compliant?

To achieve this, regulation alone is insufficient. It requires a shift in the design ethos of financial technology: from behaviour engineering to *behaviour stewardship*. From optimising for stickiness to optimising for sovereignty. The metrics must evolve—from engagement to impact, from clicks to clarity, from habit formation to value formation.

Ultimately, the line between addiction and empowerment is not fixed. It is relational. A nudge is helpful until it's coercive. A reward is motivating until it's manipulative. A habit is empowering until it becomes compulsive. In AI-mediated finance, that line is not drawn by design patterns alone, but by the values of those who create them—and the vigilance of those who use them. If we are to build systems that truly serve human flourishing, we must be willing to ask, again and again, not just *what works*, but *what matters*.

The New Currency: Attention

If capital once flowed to those with land, then to those with labour, and later to those with data, it now quietly flows to those who can capture attention. Not just momentary focus, but sustained, patterned, monetisable attention. Financial technology, long preoccupied with returns and risk, is now learning what the social platforms already know: *attention is leverage*. In the age of financial AI, this shift is redefining what counts as value—and recasting cognitive bandwidth as a scarce economic resource.

To understand this shift, consider how AI-driven financial systems are designed. Their value propositions depend not just on delivering better returns or more efficient services, but on maintaining a relationship with the user. Robo-advisors, savings apps, credit monitoring tools, and embedded financial widgets all operate on engagement loops—each one carefully calibrated to optimise not only the flow of capital, but the flow of *focus*. The result is an increasingly symbiotic relationship between financial behaviour and digital attentiveness. One informs, shapes, and constrains the other.

Traditional finance presumed that users were intermittently attentive. You might check your investments quarterly, review your budget monthly, speak to an advisor annually. But today's systems are engineered for *persistent micro-engagement*. The behavioural prompt is constant: a notification about your spending trend this week, an alert about a dip in your ETF, a gamified suggestion to contribute to a new savings goal. These nudges are not just convenient—they are strategic. They convert attention into data, data into prediction, prediction into product targeting. And every interaction adds weight to the model's understanding of how to keep you engaged.

This realignment is not accidental. It follows the logic of the attention economy, which has already transformed media, retail, and communication. Platforms that dominate user time also dominate the market. In fintech, this logic introduces a subtle reorientation: the metric of success shifts from wealth accumulation to user retention. The core question is no longer "Did the user grow their portfolio?" but "Did the user return to the app three times this week?" If engagement becomes the key performance indicator, financial systems begin to adopt the design priorities of consumer tech—reward mechanisms, behavioural loops, A/B tested friction points—all optimised to capture more of the user's cognitive space.

This has direct implications for financial behaviour. Users are encouraged to make more frequent decisions, even when infrequent, strategic ones would be more appropriate. Consider trading apps that frame each session as an opportunity to make moves—"Today's

Top Movers," "What Your Peers Are Buying," "Markets Are Down—Act Now." The premise is that financial vigilance is empowerment. But this perpetual attention does not always yield better outcomes. Studies consistently show that overtrading erodes returns, that frequent monitoring increases anxiety, and that reactive behaviours—however well-informed—undermine long-term strategy. Yet the system incentivises precisely these habits because they drive platform activity.

In this model, *attention is not just the means; it is the monetisable outcome.* A user who logs in daily generates more behavioural data, which refines personalisation algorithms, which in turn increase stickiness and monetisation potential. The user becomes not only the customer but also the product—an insight already familiar in ad-driven tech but now embedded into the infrastructure of financial life. And when financial decisions are shaped within this dynamic, it becomes difficult to distinguish between autonomy and influence.

What makes this shift particularly complex is that attention is both finite and unevenly distributed. A financially literate professional with time and resources may treat engagement as strategic. But someone with cognitive overload—a gig worker balancing multiple apps, a parent navigating economic insecurity, an individual living with chronic stress—may find that constant prompts exacerbate fatigue rather than foster clarity. The system may be optimised for attentiveness, but *not everyone has attention to spare.* In such cases, financial AI can inadvertently widen inequalities—not through access, but through attention asymmetry.

This also intersects with the notion of *financial bandwidth*, a term increasingly used to describe the mental capacity available for managing money effectively. Research in behavioural economics has shown that scarcity—not just of money, but of cognitive space—alters decision-making. When people are mentally overloaded, they make more short-term decisions, discount future rewards, and are more susceptible to nudges. A platform designed to maximise engagement in such contexts may end up reinforcing volatility rather than stability. The user appears active, but is in fact *reactive*, trapped in a loop of immediate response with limited space for reflective planning.

In this light, attention must be seen not merely as a behavioural metric but as a *moral and design consideration.* Platforms that rely on AI-driven personalisation have a responsibility to interrogate *what kind of attention* they are capturing. Is it voluntary or habitual? Is it empowering or draining? Is the user becoming more aware, or more dependent? These are not just user experience questions—they are questions of agency, dignity, and cognitive justice.

Some fintech designers are beginning to explore alternative paradigms. Instead of defaulting to high-frequency interaction, a growing minority of apps now promote *intentional minimalism.* For example, the savings app YNAB (You Need a Budget) encourages users to spend less time in the app once they've built habits, using scheduled planning sessions rather than constant updates. Others offer "focus modes" that limit notifications and explicitly discourage reactive behaviour during market turbulence. These designs honour attention not as a commodity, but as a stewardship responsibility—something to be protected, not merely harvested.

There is also the potential for new financial literacy frameworks that incorporate attention as a core component. It's no longer enough to understand compound interest or debt ratios. Users must be taught to recognise when their attention is being monetised, how interface design influences perception, and how to establish boundaries between financial awareness and financial obsession. This kind of literacy equips individuals not just to use tools effectively, but to *resist being used by them.*

At a systemic level, this reframing of attention has implications for how we evaluate the performance and ethics of AI in finance. Traditional audits of algorithmic fairness focus on bias in lending, access, or pricing. But what about *attentional fairness*? Should platforms be evaluated based on how equitably they distribute cognitive demands? Should regulators consider metrics like user fatigue, interface overload, or emotional impact alongside APRs and transparency disclosures? These are not esoteric concerns. They are grounded in a recognition that *what we attend to shapes what we become*—and that any system which governs attention governs aspiration, strategy, and ultimately, wellbeing.

The convergence of financial AI and the attention economy represents one of the most under-acknowledged shifts in modern finance. It transforms money management from a domain of periodic decision-making into a continuous behavioural stream. It turns dashboards into dopamine engines and planning into performance. And while it offers remarkable tools for personalisation and accessibility, it also introduces subtle pressures that can erode reflection, induce fatigue, and undermine the very autonomy financial planning is meant to protect.

To build systems that truly serve human flourishing, we must ask not only *what users do*, but *why they're doing it.* Not only how often they check the app, but what that frequency reflects about their state of mind, their sense of control, and their emotional resilience. Because attention, like time and trust, is a finite resource. And in the emerging economy of financial intelligence, it may well be the most valuable currency of all.

Chapter 3
The Machine as Mentor

Once, financial advice was inseparable from the human voice. It arrived across polished desks, in hushed phone calls, or over the steadying presence of someone who knew your story as well as your balance sheet. An advisor was rarely just a technician; they were confidant, coach, at times even therapist. Advice grew from the tension between numbers and narratives, risk models and life ambitions. Today, however, the terrain looks different. Artificial intelligence has stepped from the back office into the spotlight, offering insights and predictions once thought the preserve of human judgement. What is unfolding is not merely a shift in tools, but a reordering of authority. Which leaves us asking: if machines can now analyse, forecast, and recommend, what is left that belongs uniquely to the human advisor?

The question deserves more than the tired "man versus machine" framing. This is not extinction, but co-evolution. AI does not spell the end of advice—it signals the end of the advisor whose value lay chiefly in access to data or mathematical finesse. Algorithms have absorbed that role and perform it at a scale and accuracy no person can equal. Portfolio optimisation, tax scenarios, retirement projections—these are generated in moments, endlessly updated to mirror markets and behaviour. What the machine offers is not only efficiency but augmentation. Hours of modelling collapse into seconds. Yet the outputs, however precise, still need context. They must be interpreted, challenged, woven into a story that resonates with a client's actual life. That act of translation—human, ethical, irreducibly personal—remains.

AI can simulate empathy, but it cannot inhabit it. It can register sentiment, but it cannot linger in the awkward silence of uncertainty, or carry the weight of conversations about shame, family obligation, or the fragile sense of "enough." These are not rare digressions; they are the fabric of advisory work. As money grows abstract, the emotions tied to it multiply. Clients no longer seek returns alone—they seek coherence, the alignment of values, habits, and goals. And coherence cannot be automated. It is something created together, through dialogue and trust.

Trust itself is changing shape. Where it once rested on personal reputation, credentials, or long acquaintance, it is now engineered systemically—through interfaces, disclosures, and defaults. Platforms cultivate trust not through warmth, but through architecture: risk dashboards, explainability reports, permissions settings. For users without an advisor, these tools matter greatly. Yet they also blur the question: when the system recommends, are we meant to treat it as objective? Should it be challenged? Do users understand its logic, or do they defer because the machine appears authoritative?

Here lies a new task for the human advisor: interpreter of algorithms. Not simply validator, but guide to the hidden assumptions coded into recommendations. Why this suggestion for early retirement? Which expectations about health or family does it rely upon? When is it wiser to override? These questions form the frontier of modern advice. The advisor becomes philosopher as much as planner—someone fluent in both the logic of the model and the unruly logic of the human heart.

This shift demands more than technical fluency. It calls for emotional literacy. The once-niche field of financial therapy is edging into the mainstream, precisely because money is rarely rational. Behaviour is saturated with history, memory, and identity. A refusal to save may trace back to childhood scarcity; an obsessive urge to invest may mask anxiety about legacy or belonging. Algorithms can flag anomalies. They cannot ask why. They cannot pause a session to sit with grief. They cannot discern when the wisest act is not portfolio reallocation but acknowledgment of a client's divorce, their caregiving burden, their uncertain transition. Empathy, in this sense, is not a missing feature—it is a frontier of human relevance.

Advisors, however, must also cultivate trust with the machine itself. That means knowing where its limits lie. No model is neutral. Each is built on assumptions—what risk counts as tolerable, what horizon defines success. A model trained on skewed data may reproduce systemic inequities. An algorithm penalising irregular income streams may be statistically defensible, yet ethically troubling. Advisors must see these biases, have the courage to resist them, and sometimes argue against the system in defence of the client.

This advocacy stretches into the broader architecture of digital finance. Clients must navigate permissions, privacy clauses, data policies—issues they rarely grasp unaided. What does it mean to share live transaction data? How will behaviour be folded into predictive engines for others? At what point does convenience shade into surveillance? These are not peripheral questions; they cut to the heart of financial sovereignty in an AI age. Advisors must step forward, not as technophobes but as humanisers—translating systems back into life.

That humanising work is, ultimately, the crux. What we are watching is not replacement, but division of labour: machines excelling at computation, humans specialising in meaning. The advisor of the future will not win by out-calculating an algorithm. They will remain vital by asking: "What does this output mean for the life you're striving to build?" That is not a question code can answer.

In the chapters that follow, we examine this transformation across four dimensions: first, the myth and reality of AI as replacement; second, the advisor as interpreter rather than competitor; third, the rising centrality of emotional intelligence and financial therapy; and finally, the architecture of engineered trust—how design now shapes authority, and why transparency and consent must anchor it.

Together, these currents suggest a realignment: advice moving from prescription to partnership. The machine can model probabilities. The advisor can illuminate meaning. The client, always, chooses the path worth taking. That triad is not a hierarchy. It is an ecosystem. And the future of financial planning rests on learning how to live within it, wisely and well.

Will AI Replace Financial Advisors?

It is tempting to reduce complex shifts in technology to binary outcomes—replacement or survival, disruption or obsolescence.

Few questions capture this tension more acutely than the role of financial advisors in an age of artificial intelligence. As machine learning systems begin to offer clients hyper-personalised recommendations, execute real-time portfolio adjustments, and simulate long-term financial scenarios with staggering speed, a pervasive anxiety arises: *If the machine can do all this, what's left for the human advisor?* Beneath the surface of this question lies a more consequential one—not just about jobs, but about the nature of trust, judgement, and emotional intelligence in financial life. The answer is not a simple matter of technical displacement. It is a reconfiguration of the advisory role itself—from calculator to counsellor, from strategist to steward of meaning.

To assess whether AI will replace financial advisors, we must first clarify what "replacement" would entail. If we define it purely in terms of data processing, calculation, or optimisation, then the case for automation is compelling. AI systems now routinely outperform human advisors in areas such as tax-loss harvesting, asset allocation based on modern portfolio theory, risk tolerance modelling, and fee compression through automation. These are not marginal improvements—they represent a leap in efficiency and scalability. A robo-advisor platform like Betterment or Wealthfront can manage millions of accounts simultaneously, using algorithms that adapt to market conditions faster than any human team ever could. In emerging markets, mobile-first fintech tools are delivering sophisticated planning features to users who might never access a traditional advisor—democratising access to tools once reserved for institutional clients.

But technical capability is not the same as human capacity. While machines can increasingly simulate cognitive tasks—analysing data, detecting patterns, generating forecasts—they do not *understand* in the way humans do. They do not interpret nuance, context, or emotional subtext. They do not ask "why now?" or "how does this fit into the broader life story of the client?" In short, AI excels at answers; advisors specialise in questions. And the quality of those questions is what transforms information into insight.

Consider a typical client interaction. A 50-year-old entrepreneur wants to exit their business within the next five years and asks for a retirement plan. A machine can model scenarios: varying investment returns, tax structures, withdrawal rates. But only a human advisor can read between the lines to recognise that what the client truly seeks is not a number, but a new identity. Retirement here is not a financial event; it is an existential transition. The client is not merely asking, "Do I have enough?" but "Who will I be after this?" That layer of inquiry—subtle, relational, and psychologically complex—is where the advisor becomes indispensable. Machines can process preferences, but they do not sit with *ambivalence.* And financial planning, at its core, is about managing both numbers and narratives.

This does not mean advisors are immune to displacement. Those whose value lies primarily in manual calculations or commodified product advice will find themselves increasingly undercut by AI tools. Fee compression in the advisory industry is not just about cost—it is about clarity. When clients can get 80% of their planning needs met through intelligent interfaces, they are less willing to pay premium fees for services they perceive as replicable. But this shift creates space—perhaps even urgency—for advisors to reposition themselves as *interpreters of intelligence*, not just providers of it. Their new value lies in helping clients understand not just *what* to do, but *why it matters*, and how it connects to a life well lived.

This redefinition of the advisory role also introduces new responsibilities. Advisors must now engage with algorithmic outputs in much the same way that physicians engage with diagnostic tools—neither blindly accepting nor rejecting them, but contextualising them within a broader frame. When a machine recommends a specific portfolio rebalancing based on market conditions and user risk profile, the advisor must evaluate: does this make sense given the client's recent divorce? Is the model correctly accounting for the emotional volatility that may accompany sudden wealth? Has it misread risk tolerance because of short-term behavioural data? These are not hypothetical concerns—they are *design challenges*, and advisors must become fluent in identifying both the strengths and blind spots of AI recommendations.

One critical area where this fluency becomes essential is behavioural bias. Ironically, many AI systems are designed to correct for human irrationality—smoothing emotional reactivity, enforcing disciplined contributions, automating diversification. But the models themselves are not free of bias. They reflect the data they are trained on, and that data often encodes structural inequalities or outdated assumptions. A model trained predominantly on male users with high income stability may underperform for users with intermittent earnings or caregiving responsibilities. An advisor who defers entirely to such a model without questioning its premises risks reinforcing systemic gaps under the guise of objectivity.

What's more, clients themselves are often unaware of how much agency they are ceding to the machine. A platform might present a recommended savings rate or asset mix with a confidence score and colour-coded interface, creating the illusion of precision and certainty. But very few clients know what assumptions underpin those outputs—what inflation model was used? How is volatility calculated? What scenario stressors were excluded? The advisor's role, then, is to restore *epistemic humility*—to remind clients (and sometimes themselves) that every model is a map, not the terrain. That trust in technology must be earned, not assumed.

Perhaps the most profound implication of AI's advance in finance is what it reveals about the changing nature of trust. In the traditional model, trust was personal and cumulative—it was built over time through consistent, human interactions. In the AI-infused model, trust is increasingly *procedural*. It is engineered through interface design, explainability protocols, audit trails, and algorithmic transparency. Advisors now operate within this hybrid trust environment. They must not only *be* trustworthy themselves but also act as *trust translators* between clients and the systems they rely on.

Some critics argue that the growing reliance on technology erodes the human element of financial advice, reducing it to a technocratic exercise. But this critique misunderstands the opportunity. The more that machines handle routine complexity, the more space there is for humans to address existential complexity. AI may manage the mechanics of wealth, but only humans can navigate its meaning. And meaning is where most financial decisions actually live. People rarely ask for financial advice because they don't know how to add. They ask because they're navigating divorce, inheritance, career transition, or a desire to live differently. These moments require *perspective*, not just precision.

The future of financial advising, then, is not a matter of resisting AI, but of *redefining excellence within its presence.* Advisors who thrive will be those who can synthesise algorithmic intelligence with emotional insight—who can explain not just what the model suggests, but why a client might (or might not) follow it. They will need new skills: conversational depth, narrative thinking, digital ethics, systems literacy. They will become guides not just for money, but for meaning.

The real question, therefore, is not whether AI will replace financial advisors. It is whether advisors will evolve fast enough to remain irreplaceable—not through competition with machines, but through *complementarity* with them. The advisor of the future will not simply calculate returns. They will curate lives. They will design meaning. And they will help their clients navigate one of the most complex questions of our age: not "What can I afford?" but "What is worth building—and how do I stay human in the process?"

Advising the Algorithm

For generations, the financial advisor's authority rested on two assets: access to information and the ability to interpret it. In a world of scarcity—where market data was obscure, modelling tools were expensive, and investment strategies were protected behind institutional walls—advisors were indispensable as both gatekeepers and guides. That world is now vanishing. Artificial intelligence, with its unparalleled capacity to absorb, process, and act upon financial data in real time, has dramatically flattened the informational hierarchy. Clients no longer come to advisors because they lack access to insights; they come overwhelmed by abundance. The core question has shifted from *what* to do, to *how to make sense of what the machine says we should do*. The advisor's new role is not to outperform the algorithm, but to *advise the algorithm*—to understand, critique, and translate its outputs with wisdom, context, and ethical clarity.

This evolution demands a cognitive pivot. Most advisors were trained in the traditions of numerical literacy, market history, and financial regulation. They mastered balance sheets, return projections, and portfolio theory. But AI does not operate within those static paradigms. It adapts, evolves, and often reveals non-obvious correlations that defy classical intuition. This doesn't make it smarter; it makes it *different.* Advising in this context is less about proving the algorithm wrong and more about understanding *how it reached its conclusion*, what assumptions underlie it, and whether those assumptions align with the client's values and lived reality.

Take, for example, a client presented with an AI-generated retirement strategy that recommends deferring home ownership in favour of higher equity exposure. The model has calculated this based on income volatility, age, risk profile, and long-term capital market assumptions. It is technically defensible, mathematically elegant—and emotionally tone-deaf. The client may have inherited strong cultural beliefs about the importance of home ownership, or carry trauma from housing insecurity in childhood. These are not inputs the algorithm recognises, but they profoundly affect decision-making. The advisor's job is to hold space for that dissonance, to articulate the trade-offs, and—crucially—to teach the client *how to push back* when the machine is misaligned with the human.

That act of teaching is now central. The relationship between humans and AI in finance cannot be one of passive acceptance. Left unexamined, machine outputs can easily harden into de facto rules, especially when dressed in the language of precision—probability bands, heat maps, predictive scores. But every algorithm carries a worldview. It is trained on historical data, filtered through design choices, and shaped by implicit goals. Some prioritise maximising returns; others balance risk-adjusted benchmarks. Some overvalue short-term behavioural cues; others ignore emotional nuance altogether. Advisors must therefore evolve from being mere purveyors of financial advice to *critical literates of machine logic*—able to interrogate the recommendations, interpret their implications, and educate clients on where discretion remains not just possible, but essential.

Consider the analogy of modern medicine. A doctor does not reject diagnostic algorithms; they rely on them to improve accuracy. But they also know that a diagnosis must be *delivered*, not just computed. It must be placed in a narrative, discussed with empathy, adjusted for patient preferences. Likewise, financial advisors must learn to *deliver* algorithmic advice—not just accept it wholesale or dismiss it blindly, but offer a layered understanding of what it means. They must learn to say: "This recommendation makes sense statistically, but given your family goals and stress levels, we might weight stability over growth here." That layer of discretion is not a rejection of AI; it is a *refinement* of it.

This responsibility becomes even more pronounced when we consider the increasing opacity of machine learning models. Many of the most powerful financial algorithms today operate as "black boxes"—neural networks whose internal logic is too complex for direct human interpretation. While explainable AI (XAI) is a growing field, it is still far from universally implemented in consumer-facing fintech. Advisors are often left interpreting outputs without full access to the underlying logic. In this context, *interpretation becomes an act of ethical mediation.* Advisors must be prepared to say not just "here's what the model suggests," but "here's what we don't know about how the model arrived there." Transparency, or the lack thereof, becomes a factor in the advisory process.

Moreover, financial advisors must now navigate a dual-trust ecosystem. Traditionally, clients evaluated the *advisor's* trustworthiness. Increasingly, they must also decide whether to trust *the system*—the app, the algorithm, the dashboard. And those systems are designed to elicit trust by mimicking human fluency: intuitive interfaces, confidence scores, visualised outcomes. But trust by design is not always trust by merit. Just as a well-dressed con artist may appear more trustworthy than a dishevelled sage, a sleek algorithm can obscure weak assumptions. Advisors must help clients differentiate between *aesthetic confidence* and *functional reliability*—a skill that is rarely taught but increasingly urgent.

This shift is not without tension. Many advisors feel an implicit threat in the rise of AI—a fear that their value will diminish as machines improve. But this view underestimates the human demand for *coherence*. Clients do not merely want good outcomes; they want to *understand* their outcomes. They want a sense of continuity between their values and their decisions. And they want someone to accompany them in uncertainty—not just automate it away. AI excels at simulating certainty; humans excel at managing ambiguity. The advisor's role is not less relevant in this context; it is *more necessary than ever*.

However, maintaining relevance will require a retooling of both mindset and skillset. Advisors must become fluent in algorithmic logic, probabilistic reasoning, and ethical trade-off analysis. They must learn to operate in a space where definitive answers are rare, and where their primary contribution is *judgement*, not just knowledge. This is not about becoming programmers or data scientists. It is about becoming *translators*—professionals who can bridge the gap between machine precision and human complexity.

The future of financial advice is not a choice between humans and machines. It is a recalibration of roles. The machine can monitor, model, and suggest. The advisor must contextualise, interpret, and coach. This symbiosis is not automatic; it must be cultivated with care. If done well, it opens the possibility for a new kind of advisory practice—one that is not reactive, but reflective; not driven by transaction, but by transformation.

In this emerging paradigm, the most valuable advisors will not be those who offer the best predictions, but those who facilitate the most *meaningful decisions*. They will not just answer the question, "What should I do?" but help clients ask, "What kind of life do I want to build—and how does this decision support that?" Advising the algorithm, then, is not just about understanding the machine. It is about deepening our understanding of each other, and of the values that lie beneath every financial choice.

Financial Therapy in the Age of AI

At the intersection of finance and psychology lies an uncomfortable truth: many people do not make poor financial decisions because they lack information, but because they are entangled in emotional patterns they cannot articulate. Shame around debt, anxiety over spending, the deep-seated fear of running out, the compulsive urge to accumulate—these are not data problems; they are human problems. Yet, the financial industry has historically been structured to treat money as a purely rational domain, where logic governs choice and numbers tell the whole story. This illusion is now unraveling. As AI systems increasingly handle the technical elements of financial planning, what remains in the advisor's domain is not less important—it is more human. The future of financial wellness will be built not only on algorithms, but on *empathy*. And this marks the quiet rise of a new professional identity: the financial therapist.

The concept of financial therapy may sound soft to those schooled in classical economics, but it is grounded in a growing body of research that links emotional well-being to financial behaviour. Studies in behavioural finance, neuroeconomics, and clinical psychology repeatedly demonstrate that our attitudes toward money are shaped early, often unconsciously, and persistently influence our actions—regardless of income or education. Someone who grew up in a household where scarcity was the norm may develop hoarding tendencies or anxiety around investing. Another raised in an environment where money equalled status might chase high-risk opportunities to fulfil a need for validation. These patterns are not always irrational—they are *contextually rational* responses to emotional conditioning. And no spreadsheet, no matter how advanced, can parse them without compassionate inquiry.

This is precisely where AI encounters its most profound limitation. It can detect anomalies, surface insights, and optimise portfolios with astonishing speed. It can predict when someone is likely to miss a payment or flag unusual transactions. But it cannot ask, "How do you feel when you think about your financial future?" It cannot notice the hesitation in a client's voice, or the relief that flickers across their face when a debt strategy is explained in plain language. Emotional resonance is not a data point—it is an *experience*. And this is where human advisors, trained in financial therapy principles, become not just relevant, but essential.

The role of financial advisors is undergoing a metamorphosis. No longer merely custodians of wealth, they are being called to serve as stewards of well-being. In this new paradigm, technical competence is a baseline, not a differentiator. What sets a modern advisor apart is their ability to hold emotionally charged conversations about money without judgment, to unpack limiting beliefs, to guide clients through financial trauma with sensitivity. This does not mean becoming a psychologist. Rather, it means acknowledging that every financial decision is, at its core, a human decision—and that human decisions are rarely made in a vacuum of pure reason.

Consider a young professional with high income but mounting credit card debt. Traditional advice might involve setting a budget and reducing discretionary spending. An AI assistant might recommend the same based on historical spending patterns. But a financial therapist would probe deeper: Why is this person spending beyond their means? Is it a response to workplace stress, loneliness, or an unconscious drive to impress peers? Addressing these root causes may require reframing their financial identity, not just correcting behaviour. Without that level of engagement, even the best financial plan is fragile—because it does not speak to the person *behind* the numbers.

Financial therapy is particularly vital in life transitions, where uncertainty meets emotion: divorce, death, inheritance, retirement. These are periods where people are least capable of making objective decisions, and most vulnerable to reactive or fear-driven choices. AI may be able to suggest optimal paths, but it cannot sit with someone in grief, nor interpret the unique emotional weight that money carries during such times. Human advisors, trained in active listening, somatic awareness, and values-based inquiry, can help clients navigate these crossroads with clarity and dignity.

The convergence of AI and financial therapy also presents ethical tensions. As robo-advisors and smart apps begin to incorporate behavioural nudges—rewarding saving behaviour, gamifying investing, automating bill payments—they blur the line between *assistance* and *manipulation.* Are users being empowered, or subtly coerced? Financial therapy equips professionals to interrogate this boundary. It asks: Is this recommendation serving the client's stated values, or merely the platform's growth metrics? Is the nudge improving behaviour sustainably, or creating dependence? The therapeutic lens demands not only better outcomes, but *healthier processes.*

Real-world applications are emerging across the financial sector. Some advisory firms now integrate licensed therapists into planning meetings. Others train advisors in tools like money scripts, genograms, and motivational interviewing to uncover clients' inherited narratives around wealth. Digital platforms are experimenting with emotionally intelligent chatbots that respond to user sentiment, though these remain rudimentary. The trend is clear: financial services are no longer just about transactions—they are about transformation. And that transformation requires emotional intelligence at scale.

This shift also invites a more expansive definition of wealth. Mental wellness, social capital, and personal meaning are increasingly recognised as integral to financial health. A client may have a technically optimal plan but still feel unfulfilled. Perhaps they are investing in markets that conflict with their ethics, or deferring enjoyment out of fear. Financial therapy allows for conversations that do not reduce success to net worth, but expand it to include peace of mind, alignment with purpose, and freedom from anxiety. These are outcomes no algorithm can deliver—but which many clients silently crave.

For financial professionals, embracing this shift involves more than adopting a new skillset; it demands a new mindset. One that sees the client not as a balance sheet, but as a complex emotional being. One that understands that numbers are never neutral, and that every financial behaviour tells a story. One that values *presence* as much as precision. This is not softening the profession—it is *maturing* it.

At a broader level, the integration of emotional intelligence into financial practice reflects a cultural awakening. As societies grapple with burnout, inequality, and the psychological costs of hypercapitalism, there is growing recognition that money is not just a tool but a mirror. It reflects our hopes, fears, values, and vulnerabilities. Financial therapy holds up that mirror with compassion, helping clients see themselves not as flawed decision-makers, but as meaning-makers navigating a complex world.

And this is where the human advisor has something irreplaceable to offer. Not superior forecasting. Not faster calculations. But *connection*. In an industry seduced by automation, the most radical thing a professional can offer is attention—undistracted, empathetic, and curious. The irony of AI is that the more it handles the mechanics, the more it exposes the emotional core of financial life. And in that space, only another human can truly meet us.

As artificial intelligence takes over the tasks that are cold and calculable, it leaves behind what is warm and unquantifiable. Financial therapy is not a fringe practice—it is the frontier. And those who embrace it will not only build better plans. They will build deeper trust, foster greater well-being, and help redefine what it means to be truly "wealthy" in a machine-augmented world.

Trust by Design

Trust has always been the bedrock of financial systems. Banks rely on it to attract deposits. Investment firms depend on it to manage client wealth. Insurance companies cannot function without it. Yet trust, historically, has been built on human relationships and institutional reputation. We trusted the banker because we knew her by name. We believed in the financial advisor because we saw his experience etched into every well-reasoned plan. These relationships were not infallible, but they were legible—they gave us someone to blame, someone to call, someone who could explain. As artificial intelligence takes a larger role in financial planning and decision-making, this legibility is disappearing. In its place, a new architecture of trust is being assembled—not through handshakes and heritage, but through *design*.

The issue is not simply technological. It is philosophical. Traditional financial systems ask us to trust *people* using tools. AI-infused systems ask us to trust *tools* making decisions that affect people. That reversal of agency introduces a new set of risks, particularly when those tools are opaque, proprietary, or poorly understood. Algorithms are now recommending investments, approving loans, flagging suspicious activity, and even coaching users on financial behaviour. Yet many users do not know how these systems work, what data they are using, or on what basis they are making recommendations. This black-box phenomenon undermines confidence. And it is here that the concept of *trust by design* becomes both necessary and urgent.

Trust by design is not a slogan. It is an emerging discipline that seeks to embed explainability, transparency, fairness, and consent into the architecture of financial technology. In contrast to the default "trust us" model of legacy institutions or the "don't ask, just automate" ethos of some tech platforms, trust by design insists that users must be able to understand, evaluate, and influence the systems they rely on. In the context of AI-powered finance, that means building systems that are not only accurate, but *accountable*—and that communicate their logic in ways that non-specialists can grasp.

One of the most critical components of this effort is *explainability*. In AI circles, this is often referred to as XAI (explainable artificial intelligence). The premise is simple: if an algorithm is making decisions that materially affect people's financial lives—whether it's assigning a credit score, adjusting a portfolio, or nudging spending behaviour—it should be able to *show its work*. But explainability is not just a technical feature; it is a design challenge. Raw code or statistical models are meaningless to most users. What's needed is narrative clarity: Why did the system make this recommendation? What factors did it weigh most heavily? How might a different choice have led to a different outcome?

Some platforms are beginning to tackle this. For example, certain robo-advisors now offer visual breakdowns of investment rationales, allowing users to see how risk tolerance, time horizon, and market conditions interact to produce a recommendation. Others allow users to adjust key assumptions and watch the model re-calculate in real time. These are early steps, but they matter. *When users understand the logic behind a decision, they are more likely to trust both the process and the outcome—even if they ultimately disagree with it.*

Transparency goes hand in hand with explainability, but it addresses a different layer: *what* the system is doing, and *why*. This includes disclosing how user data is collected, stored, and used; how machine learning models are trained; what sources of bias may be present; and what recourse is available if something goes wrong. It also means being honest about the limitations of the system. AI may be able to optimise a retirement strategy, but it cannot forecast a user's future health, marital status, or job satisfaction. Systems that overpromise—suggesting they can provide certainty in an uncertain world—risk betraying trust the moment reality intrudes.

One instructive case came from a fintech firm that used AI to recommend personalised savings goals. Users initially embraced the feature, but complaints began to emerge when it became clear that the system penalised those who deviated from its suggestions—without ever explaining why those goals were set in the first place. The company responded by adding a transparency layer: a dashboard showing users how their goals were calculated, and offering manual override options. The backlash subsided. Not because the algorithm changed, but because the *relationship* to the algorithm changed. *Transparency restored agency.*

Which brings us to perhaps the most underappreciated pillar of trust by design: *user consent.* In most financial contexts, consent is treated as a compliance formality—something to be checked off during onboarding or buried in terms and conditions. But true consent is not passive. It is informed, intentional, and revisable. Users should not only know what they are agreeing to; they should have meaningful control over how their data is used, how recommendations are generated, and how their goals are prioritised. This becomes especially important as AI systems grow more autonomous and proactive. A smart assistant that reallocates funds without notice may be technically efficient—but if it does so without consent, it can quickly erode trust, no matter how "right" the decision proves to be.

Progressive financial platforms are beginning to experiment with layered consent protocols. These include options that let users choose between default, guided, and expert modes of engagement; dynamic prompts that request approval before significant changes are made; and granular privacy settings that empower users to control data flows. Importantly, these features are not marketed as add-ons—they are presented as core components of a trustworthy experience. And that shift in framing matters. *When trust is embedded in the default settings, not merely appended at the edges, it signals respect for the user's autonomy.*

Still, the implementation of trust by design is not without complications. For one, there is an inherent tension between *efficiency* and *explainability*. Highly complex models often achieve superior predictive power, but are also less interpretable. The trade-off between performance and transparency is real—and not always easy to resolve. In high-stakes financial applications, the bias often leans toward accuracy. But as regulatory frameworks evolve and user expectations mature, pressure is growing to favour models that may be slightly less precise, but far more transparent.

There is also the issue of *power asymmetry*. Even with explainability tools and consent protocols in place, most users are still operating at a significant knowledge disadvantage compared to the system architects. This asymmetry can be exploited—subtly or overtly—through dark patterns, persuasive defaults, or data monetisation strategies that the average user does not fully grasp. Trust by design must therefore be complemented by *governance by principle*. This includes independent audits, open standards, and regulatory oversight to ensure that transparency is not performative, but substantive.

One model worth examining is the emerging field of algorithmic accountability reporting, where independent researchers and journalists evaluate AI systems for fairness, bias, and transparency. In the financial sector, this could take the form of third-party audits of robo-advisors, consumer ratings for AI-driven services, or public dashboards tracking model performance across demographic groups. These tools not only build public trust—they hold institutions accountable in ways that traditional branding or PR never could.

The broader implication is clear: *Trust is no longer a passive asset. It must be actively engineered.* This engineering is not purely technical; it is also cultural, philosophical, and relational. It requires a rethinking of what it means to build systems that are not just intelligent, but trustworthy. Systems that do not merely make good decisions, but do so in ways that respect the dignity, autonomy, and values of the people affected by them.

As financial AI continues to evolve, the institutions that thrive will not be those with the most advanced models, but those with the most trusted systems. And trust, like capital, compounds over time—when users feel seen, informed, and respected at every touchpoint. Trust by design is not a box to be ticked. It is a discipline to be cultivated. And in a world where machines increasingly manage our money, that discipline may prove to be the most valuable investment of all.

Chapter 4
Wealth Without Borders

Not long ago, investing beyond one's borders was an indulgence of the few. It required gatekeepers—international banks with their polished façades, brokers fluent in multiple currencies, legal advisers versed in cross-jurisdictional rules. Wealth itself had to be matched by stamina: the capacity to wrestle with bureaucracy and regulatory labyrinths. Now, much of that infrastructure has been compressed into a device. A teenager in Jakarta can push capital into a Silicon Valley ETF with a few taps. A freelancer in Nairobi might accept a crypto payment and, within minutes, reinvest it into a decentralised yield pool. Through AI-driven platforms, the geography of money is being remapped—not by parliaments or treaties, but by computation itself.

Artificial intelligence is dismantling the old gatekeeping structures of finance. Algorithms parse regulations, interpret market signals in real time, and move assets across borders with speeds inconceivable a decade ago. But perhaps more significant than the where is the who. A rising class of investors, free from the weight of legacy institutions, are making decisions once confined to multinationals or hedge funds. Insights no longer arrive as dense reports; they appear as context-aware nudges—tailored, digestible, adaptive to language and culture. The phrase "global investor" now fits anyone with a signal, a screen, and the nerve to risk.

Yet with expansion comes paradox. Access may be wider, but complexity has thickened. The same tools that let a designer in São Paulo dip into European equities also expose them to the churn of currency fluctuations, mismatched regulatory environments, and macroeconomic tremors far beyond sight. Risk has grown diffuse, ambient, difficult to grasp. It moves not just through markets, but through models—models whose roots lie in Silicon Valley, Singapore, or elsewhere. Which begs the question: whose interests are embedded in their code?

Global finance does not exist apart from culture. Algorithms carry the fingerprints of their makers: economic assumptions, value judgements, behavioural defaults. A robo-adviser trained on US data may tilt portfolios heavily toward equities, championing growth over caution. One built in Japan might lean towards bonds, conservative allocations, and a deflation-conscious outlook. These variations are not cosmetic. They subtly redirect goals, recalibrate risk appetites, and shape what users believe is financially prudent. Currency, in this sense, is culture; and culture, translated into code, becomes destiny.

Take attitudes to debt. In America, borrowing is often recast as leverage—fuel for expansion. In Germany, it is shaded with caution, more burden than tool. In Japan, debt has long carried a moral undertone, tinged with shame. An AI system that misreads these instincts—treating them as statistical quirks rather than deep-seated norms—risks alienation, or worse, manipulation. Cultural literacy, not just technical accuracy, is the demand of cross-border finance.

Nowhere is this more visible than among digital nomads. This swelling demographic—remote workers, crypto entrepreneurs, itinerant creatives—live without fixed anchors. Their income streams, expenses, and portfolios stretch across continents. For them, AI is indispensable. It reconciles multiple tax codes, times currency swaps, even flags geopolitical events that might nudge a reallocation. But such sophistication comes with a price: trust. And with it, a need for belonging. Traditional banks cannot accommodate clients without addresses, without national anchors. AI-native platforms can—but they require a renegotiation of the social contract.

Here lies another tension: empowerment versus inequality. In theory, AI democratises access to tools long monopolised by institutions. In practice, infrastructure mediates outcomes. Connectivity, literacy—digital and financial—determine who benefits. A machine-learning investing app might technically function in Uganda or the Philippines, but without reliable internet or regulatory protection, its promise falters. In Africa, mobile money leapfrogged banks; yet algorithmic credit scoring has also entrenched bias, excluding those with scant data histories. In Southeast Asia, fintech adoption is rampant, but with many platforms unregulated, exploitation shadows opportunity.

Access, then, is not equality. Availability does not guarantee usability. And usability does not ensure benefit. Democratisation must be tethered to localisation: intelligence that adapts to context, that speaks the financial dialects of place. AI must learn not just to calculate, but to interpret—how different societies imagine safety, risk, prosperity. Efficiency alone is insufficient. Dignity must count too.

Technically, the means exist. Federated learning allows systems to absorb local patterns without betraying privacy. Natural language models can interpret informal money practices and integrate them into formal systems. Consent protocols can be customised to reflect cultural norms about ownership and authority. Interfaces, too, can shift—from sterile minimalism to designs attuned to local aesthetics and values. The real test is not technological but institutional: will those building these systems treat inclusivity as essential, or as an afterthought?

For financial services straddling the globe, two imperatives emerge: scale without flattening, personalise without condescension. Context is not just data; it is meaning. To serve tomorrow's investor, platforms must do more than churn out optimised advice. They must grasp what money signifies in particular lives.

Because money is never neutral. It embodies fear, hope, identity. For one, wealth means legacy; for another, escape. For some it signals freedom, for others duty. AI that misses these layers will misread desires, offer ill-suited strategies, and corrode trust. But AI attuned to this diversity could be powerfully enabling—uncovering opportunities unseen, buffering risks unrecognised, aligning financial action with both global possibility and personal truth.

This chapter traces that future: how AI reconfigures participation in global markets, the cultural biases it encodes, the risks that accompany globalised data, and the moral questions of equity. It offers both cases and critique, a framework for thinking about wealth in a world where borders blur but cultural differences persist.

The real question is not whether AI will make finance swifter, sharper. That much is already given. The deeper question is whether it can make finance more just. And that, in the end, is not a matter of code at all. It is a matter of design.

AI and the Global Investor

Until recently, investing across international markets was an activity largely confined to institutions and ultra-high-net-worth individuals. It required specialised knowledge, professional intermediaries, and access to infrastructure that only the financial elite could afford. But that architecture has undergone a seismic transformation. What once necessitated a fleet of analysts, currency strategists, and regulatory consultants can now be accessed by a novice investor through a smartphone app. AI has become the great enabler—not merely flattening the terrain of access, but reconfiguring the investor profile itself. The global investor is no longer a hedge fund in Manhattan. It could just as easily be a 22-year-old coder in Lagos or a nurse in Hanoi.

AI has fundamentally changed what it means to "participate" in the global economy. With intelligent interfaces translating economic data, managing currency risk, and generating personalised portfolio suggestions in milliseconds, barriers that once segregated local investors from global opportunities have begun to dissolve. Platforms like eToro, Robinhood, and Freetrade have democratised equities; robo-advisors like Betterment and Stash have brought algorithmic portfolio management to the retail level. Beneath the surface of these apps, AI is performing an extraordinary feat: ingesting vast quantities of structured and unstructured data—geopolitical shifts, earnings forecasts, interest rate expectations, social sentiment—and compressing them into probabilistic judgments that influence investment advice for tens of millions of users.

But access is not comprehension. And comprehension is not risk mastery. While AI allows a novice investor in Mumbai to buy shares in a Singaporean logistics company or allocate funds to a renewable energy ETF listed in Oslo, it also introduces a new level of abstraction between the investor and the assets they hold. What's gained in simplicity may be lost in situational awareness. Users may follow AI-optimised recommendations without a full grasp of the economic, political, or regulatory environments underpinning those assets. AI has not made global investing easier; it has made it deceptively accessible.

This is not an indictment of the technology, but a call for greater realism. AI excels at pattern recognition, speed, and scale. It can backtest thousands of scenarios, flag volatility events, and suggest rebalancing strategies far more quickly than a human advisor. What it lacks is the ability to contextualise its own conclusions—why it favours one emerging market bond fund over another, or what structural risks it may be underweighting due to insufficient data from underrepresented economies. Novice investors often assume AI's recommendations are neutral, rational, or "correct" when, in fact, they reflect the assumptions and training data of the models they emerge from. This gives rise to a dangerous form of dependency: algorithmic trust without algorithmic literacy.

The tension between empowerment and exposure is further exacerbated by the cultural neutrality—or cultural blindness—of many AI-driven financial platforms. Investing is not just a mathematical exercise; it is a cultural behaviour. The risk appetite of a retail investor in São Paulo may differ radically from that of a counterpart in Stockholm, not merely due to economic conditions but because of social norms, historical experience, and intergenerational narratives. AI models trained predominantly on North American or Western European data may inadvertently reinforce investment behaviours that do not align with users in Southeast Asia, Sub-Saharan Africa, or the Middle East. This becomes particularly problematic when risk models are ported wholesale into new markets without adaptation.

AI's greatest strength—its ability to scale insights across geographies—can also be its greatest weakness. The algorithms that drive portfolio recommendations are increasingly designed to optimise for general outcomes across heterogeneous user bases. But financial behaviour is inherently local. Saving for a house in Jakarta is not the same as saving for one in Toronto. The timeline, inflation exposure, credit access, and real estate volatility are different—and so are the social pressures and expectations. An AI that fails to take these contextual variables into account may produce advice that is mathematically sound, yet practically misaligned.

There's also the question of time horizons. Institutional investors can afford to think in decades. Retail investors often think in months, or even weeks. AI-driven platforms may recommend strategies based on long-term historical data that assume user patience and capital stability—assumptions that don't hold for many gig workers, informal earners, or first-time investors dealing with economic precarity. AI may be optimising for long-term efficiency while the user is dealing with short-term survival. The dissonance between model design and user reality creates a subtle but dangerous gap in expectations, especially when losses occur and confidence erodes.

Yet there is an even more subtle shift underway—one that speaks not to what investors are doing, but to *who they believe they are*. The advent of AI-guided investing has begun to reshape investor identity itself. No longer is investment seen purely as an exercise in strategy or knowledge. Increasingly, it is presented as a lifestyle—gamified, aesthetically packaged, and emotionally tethered to identity signals. Investing through platforms that use AI to micro-target preferences, suggest "trending" assets, and reward behavioural loyalty subtly reshapes users into not just participants, but *followers* of the algorithmic narrative. The investor ceases to be the author of their portfolio and becomes its audience.

This raises deeper questions about autonomy. If AI platforms are designed to minimise user effort, maximise engagement, and reinforce behaviour that aligns with platform success metrics (e.g. retention, transaction volume), what happens to the idea of informed consent in financial decision-making? AI may be making recommendations, but are users really making decisions? When the line between advice and automation blurs, so too does the notion of responsibility. If a retail investor loses money following an AI-guided path, who is accountable—the user, the designer, or the model itself?

One path forward is not to reject AI-guided investing, but to reframe it. AI should not be treated as an oracle, but as an advisor whose output demands interpretation. Just as one would interrogate the assumptions behind a human financial planner's recommendations, so too should we interrogate the logic of machine-generated strategies. What data is being used? What markets are being prioritised? What risks are being excluded because they are too complex to model? Financial literacy in the age of AI must evolve to include algorithmic literacy—a functional understanding of how financial models make decisions, and what their blind spots might be.

Equally, platform designers must embed explainability into the architecture of financial AI. Users must be able to ask *why*—why this fund, why now, why this level of risk—and receive answers that are not obscured by layers of technical jargon or vague generalities. Visual explanations, contextual warnings, and plain-language rationale must become standard. The democratization of investment should not come at the cost of transparency.

Ultimately, AI is neither saviour nor saboteur. It is a multiplier. It amplifies the intelligence of the infrastructure it is embedded within, and the intentions of those who design it. Used well, it can offer the novice investor unprecedented access to the tools, markets, and strategies that have historically been out of reach. It can guide decisions that are informed, adaptive, and strategically sound. Used poorly, it can disguise risk, oversimplify complexity, and lull users into passive dependence.

The global investor is no longer an abstraction. It is a lived reality, enabled by AI but defined by design. The challenge now is not whether AI will open new markets—it already has. The challenge is whether those markets will be navigable, ethical, and aligned with the lived realities of those newly entering them. In the coming years, the most important financial decisions may not be made by traders in towers, but by ordinary people in ordinary homes, advised by invisible algorithms that never sleep. The quality of those decisions will depend not on the intelligence of the machines, but on the wisdom of the systems we build around them.

Digital Nomads, Digital Assets

The economic passport once defined where a person could live, earn, and invest. Today, for a growing class of workers, that logic has collapsed. The traditional scaffolding of national employment, centralised banking, and localised financial regulation no longer neatly applies to a borderless workforce of digital nomads, remote freelancers, and crypto-native entrepreneurs. These individuals navigate income, expenses, and investment not in local currencies alone but in decentralised tokens, stablecoins, and multi-jurisdictional digital platforms. In this new geography of money, artificial intelligence is becoming not just a convenience but an essential infrastructure—translating complexity into actionable strategy, smoothing frictions in a multi-currency life, and redefining what it means to participate in a global economy without borders.

This demographic—what some economists term the "sovereign individual class"—challenges legacy assumptions about how wealth is earned and held. A software developer in Nairobi can bill clients in Singapore, get paid in USDC, convert it into local currency or crypto on a decentralised exchange, and park earnings in a robo-managed portfolio optimised for tax efficiency across three continents. AI handles much of this complexity behind the scenes. Intelligent interfaces parse tax treaties, currency risks, expense trends, and asset allocation—all in real-time, tailored to a lifestyle that doesn't anchor itself to one city, job, or regulatory regime. For these users, financial AI isn't merely a productivity tool; it's a survival necessity in an economic environment that is fast, fluid, and fragmented.

The emergence of this borderless economy was accelerated by a convergence of forces. The pandemic normalised remote work at scale. Cryptocurrency markets introduced alternatives to national currencies and traditional financial systems. Fintech apps like Wise, Revolut, and Deel embedded cross-border financial services into sleek user experiences. And AI, powered by advanced machine learning, made this all functionally seamless—classifying receipts from different tax codes, predicting local inflation trends, auto-adjusting savings targets based on projected earnings, and delivering investment suggestions tailored to the user's unique mobility pattern.

AI doesn't just observe financial behaviour; it increasingly anticipates it, adapting to lifestyles where volatility is constant and stability is self-authored.

Yet while AI empowers this freedom, it also obfuscates the infrastructure behind it. The more seamless the interface, the less visible the complexity—and the greater the risk of false confidence. The digital nomad may rely on a chatbot for tax advice or portfolio strategy without fully understanding the regulatory implications of operating in multiple jurisdictions. AI's smooth delivery of financial insight often conceals the layers of legal and ethical uncertainty it glosses over. Should one pay taxes in their country of origin, country of residence, or both? Is an asset held in DeFi exempt from reporting obligations? How should pension contributions be managed without a traditional employer? These are not abstract questions—they are daily dilemmas for borderless earners, and ones that AI is increasingly being asked to answer, often without transparency about the limits of its recommendations.

What makes the challenge more urgent is the rate at which this population is growing—and diversifying. No longer limited to Western freelancers or tech-savvy entrepreneurs, the digitally borderless now include remote educators in the Philippines, content creators in Colombia, and microservice developers in Pakistan. Platforms like Upwork, Fiverr, and Toptal have globalised the supply of skills, while stablecoins like USDC and DAI have globalised the store of value. AI bridges these worlds—automating invoicing in one currency and remittance in another, identifying optimal payment routes across centralised and decentralised platforms, and detecting fraud patterns invisible to human accountants. The financial lives of these users span jurisdictions, time zones, and asset classes, and AI operates as the connective tissue that keeps their economic engines running.

But this new normal presents an ideological dilemma as well: What is the role of the state in the life of a citizen who no longer relies on it for employment, banking, or retirement? The traditional social contract—labour for wages, wages taxed to fund social protection—relies on physical rootedness. The digital nomad disrupts this compact, often unintentionally, by opting out of national systems that are designed to be territorial. AI is inadvertently complicit in this shift. By offering frictionless solutions for cross-border earnings and decentralised savings, it enables users to bypass the formal systems meant to provide collective security. The consequences are not trivial: underfunded public services, eroded tax bases, and regulatory blind spots that allow wealth to move faster than oversight can follow.

There's also a deeper cognitive shift underway. For the traditional employee, finance is a linear affair—earn, save, invest, retire. For the borderless worker, finance is a dynamic equilibrium—juggling currencies, converting assets, timing exits, reallocating across jurisdictions, and managing exposure to both market and political risk. AI becomes a kind of financial exoskeleton, constantly scanning, learning, and adapting. Yet with each added layer of automation, questions of trust and agency resurface. When a financial AI decides to shift savings from a Euro-based portfolio to a DeFi yield aggregator, is that user-led strategy or AI-initiated drift? When nudges are based on models trained on high-income, Western-centric datasets, how well do they serve the reality of users in lower-income, higher-volatility environments?

One promising response is customisability. Advanced AI platforms are beginning to allow users to define their own constraints—excluding asset types, setting geo-specific rules, adjusting for personal ethics or volatility tolerance. For instance, a digital nomad who works in politically unstable regions may prioritise liquidity over yield, or decentralised assets over fiat-denominated ones. AI systems that can learn from these preferences, explain their logic, and adapt in near-real time become true collaborators rather than opaque guides. The future of AI-driven finance for the borderless class will depend not just on technical sophistication but on responsiveness to individual values and contextual nuance.

We must also consider the infrastructure gap between the digital haves and have-nots. While an Estonian digital resident can access e-governance services and bank remotely, a freelancer in Nigeria may still struggle with capital controls, unstable mobile networks, or unrecognised identity documents. AI may offer borderless capabilities, but its benefits accrue unequally based on local infrastructure, legal recognition, and access to digital tools. This is not a technological limitation but a socio-political one. Financial AI, if designed without global equity in mind, risks reinforcing exclusion even as it preaches inclusion. The solution lies in policy frameworks that adapt to this class—portable social protections, interoperable digital IDs, cross-border tax harmonisation—and in AI systems built with pluralism rather than homogenisation at their core.

There's a broader cultural shift worth noting here. The idea of financial home—once tied to a bank branch, a pension scheme, or a national currency—is being reimagined. For many digital nomads, "home" is wherever their wallet is recognised, their assets are safe, and their capital is productive. AI contributes to this redefinition by abstracting away the bureaucracy of geography. A blockchain-based property investment in Dubai, managed by an AI that rebalances the portfolio based on global interest rates and rental demand forecasts, is no longer the domain of institutional investors. It's available to individuals with an internet connection and a willingness to learn.

Still, access does not guarantee resilience. The volatility of decentralised markets, the ambiguity of legal jurisdictions, and the fragility of trust in algorithmic systems all suggest that this model of financial freedom is not without its perils. As borderless earners outsource more of their financial cognition to AI, the margin for error narrows. Systems must not only be smart; they must be accountable, explainable, and adaptable to edge cases. And users must not only be empowered but equipped—with the literacy to understand not just what AI is doing, but *why*.

Ultimately, the question is not whether AI will serve the digital nomad class—it already does. The question is how we design systems that honour their complexity without trivialising it, that scale intelligence without eroding sovereignty, and that promise efficiency without forsaking equity. For a world increasingly defined by motion rather than stability, AI offers a compass. But like all compasses, it must be read with discernment, not followed blindly. Financial citizenship, in this new paradigm, is less about where you're from and more about what tools you trust. And at the heart of those tools sits the algorithm—not as master, but as mediator in a borderless economic world still writing its rules.

Currency as Culture

Money, for all its numerical precision, is anything but neutral. It is not merely a medium of exchange or a store of value; it is also a mirror of national psychology, cultural memory, and historical trauma. How people save, spend, invest, and even discuss money is shaped by inherited narratives—some deeply rational, others quietly irrational, all powerfully formative. From the Japanese instinct to hoard cash reserves to the American comfort with revolving credit, from German inflation anxiety to Indian gold obsession, financial behaviours carry cultural DNA. Now, artificial intelligence is tasked with decoding this complex terrain—not only observing these behaviours but adapting to them, shaping them, and in some cases, challenging them. What does it mean for AI to enter the domain of culturally conditioned money habits? And can it ever be neutral in doing so?

At the heart of this question is the tension between optimisation and interpretation. AI excels at detecting patterns: it can identify that Japanese households maintain higher cash balances than their Western counterparts, or that Brazilian users are more likely to treat bonus income as disposable rather than investable. But these patterns are not mere data points—they are expressions of trust, risk appetite, intergenerational norms, and national histories. To engage responsibly with these behaviours, AI must evolve beyond statistical forecasting and develop what might be called cultural fluency. Without it, the systems that drive financial recommendations risk misalignment, even harm.

Consider the example of savings. In Japan, saving is not simply a financial act—it is a cultural virtue, tied to ideas of prudence, resilience, and societal responsibility. The country's post-war deflationary experience, combined with an ageing population and a strong collectivist ethic, has led to consistently high household savings rates. A Western-built AI model, trained on American consumer behaviour, might interpret low consumption as suboptimal and recommend increased discretionary spending or higher-risk investment portfolios. But to a Japanese user, such nudges may feel inappropriate or even reckless. Without an understanding of the underlying cultural logic, AI-driven advice can be not just ineffective, but alienating.

Contrast this with the United States, where debt is culturally normalised and even aspirational in certain contexts—seen not as a failure of restraint but as a tool for upward mobility. The American financial psyche, shaped by decades of consumerism and the ubiquity of credit instruments, leans towards optimism about future earnings and a relatively high tolerance for financial risk. An AI system interpreting American data might assume that leveraging for consumption is rational, even when personal savings are low. But applying this assumption in a culture like Germany—where memories of hyperinflation still echo and frugality remains a civic virtue—would be a fundamental misstep. There, debt carries stigma, and monetary stability is prized over consumption. A German user confronted with debt-based financial nudges would likely reject them outright, or disengage from the platform entirely.

The implications go beyond user experience—they shape how financial inclusion is defined and delivered. In India, for instance, the cultural role of gold as a store of wealth is deeply embedded, particularly among lower-income households and women. It functions as savings, insurance, and social capital all at once. A Western AI system might flag heavy investment in physical gold as inefficient or risky, failing to account for the cultural and functional logic behind it. Worse, if such a system promotes digital assets or equities without recognising the trust gap in those instruments, it could erode rather than enhance financial agency. *True financial intelligence is contextual*, not universal—and AI must be designed to respect that nuance.

This becomes particularly salient in emerging markets, where the promise of AI-driven financial tools is most celebrated. Platforms like Tala in Kenya or KoinWorks in Indonesia use AI to assess creditworthiness in the absence of traditional financial histories. On paper, this is a breakthrough for inclusion. But what assumptions underpin these models? Are they calibrated for collectivist cultures where borrowing is communal and informal, or for individualist models of liability and default? Do they interpret silence in digital behaviour as risk-averse conservatism, or as structural exclusion from digital infrastructure? The answers depend not on machine learning capacity alone, but on *cultural epistemology*—a term still largely absent from AI engineering conversations.

One proposed solution is localisation, where AI models are trained and tuned on country-specific datasets. This approach recognises that economic behaviour is not standardised across the globe, and that importing behavioural assumptions across borders can lead to dangerous generalisations. But localisation is only a start. To move toward *cultural calibration*, AI needs interpretive scaffolding: anthropological insight, linguistic nuance, and even ethical inquiry. A system that sees Chinese users' preference for family-based financial pooling must grasp not just the habit, but its Confucian roots in filial duty and intergenerational solidarity. An AI that encourages Brazilian users to set aside a portion of carnival-season bonuses must recognise that celebration, too, has financial logic—and value.

Moreover, this challenge is not just about geographic culture, but also generational and socioeconomic subcultures. Within the United Kingdom, for instance, a Gen Z gig worker in Manchester may relate to money in fundamentally different ways than a retired homeowner in Kent. One sees liquidity as optionality; the other sees it as security. For AI to serve both without stereotyping either, it must evolve from predictive recommendation engines to adaptive systems that *learn from the user*, not just about them. That requires not only better data, but better design—interfaces that allow users to correct, question, and reshape the system's assumptions about their goals and values.

The role of user feedback becomes central in this model. Today, most financial AI systems operate in a one-directional manner—observing, inferring, and nudging. But culture is not a static dataset; it is a negotiation, a conversation. Users must be able to *push back*, to explain why they hold an "inefficient" asset or refuse a "rational" refinancing offer. Systems must not only accept this friction but be designed to welcome it—treating it as signal, not noise. This is not about political correctness; it's about epistemic integrity. To offer financial advice that is genuinely intelligent, AI must become less sure of itself—and more open to being taught.

This is where explainability, often discussed in technical circles, takes on a humanist dimension. An AI that tells a user in South Korea to reduce savings and spend more must be able to *explain why*, in a way that resonates with Confucian social structures and national economic narratives. If the explanation feels foreign—devoid of local reference points, cultural symbols, or shared metaphors—the advice will not just be rejected; the entire system will lose credibility. And when trust breaks, no amount of precision will matter.

There's a broader philosophical question beneath this technical discussion: Should AI strive to harmonise global financial behaviours, or preserve cultural pluralism? The efficiency argument tends to favour harmonisation—optimising across common principles of risk-adjusted return and utility maximisation. But such models often encode Western economic norms as universal truths. Pluralism, on the other hand, embraces friction, suboptimality, and difference. It sees cultural variance not as error, but as data. Building AI that honours this view means designing systems that can *hold contradictions*—supporting high-debt lifestyles in one context and high-savings in another, without flattening either into caricature.

We may eventually need a new field altogether—*cultural AI design*—that bridges behavioural economics, design anthropology, and human-computer interaction. It would ask not just "what works?" but "what resonates?" and "what belongs?" It would test not only for efficiency but for dignity. And it would elevate financial AI from a tool of compliance to a vehicle of cultural respect.

As money becomes increasingly digital, the risk is that the systems mediating it become increasingly detached from the societies in which they operate. If culture is stripped out of financial design—if the algorithms governing our spending and saving behave as if we are all rational agents with identical goals—we will have lost something vital: the right to be economically different. The future of AI in finance, then, is not just a question of what it can compute. It's a question of what it can *understand*—and how well it can learn to listen.

The Inequality Paradox

Technology has always promised liberation. From the printing press to the smartphone, each leap has been accompanied by the hope—sometimes realised, often overstated—that access would flatten hierarchies. In financial services, artificial intelligence carries the same seduction: if algorithms can assess credit risk without prejudice, predict market trends without intermediaries, and allocate resources with mathematical objectivity, then surely inequality can be erased—or at least eroded. The problem is not that this vision is naïve. It's that it conflates access with equity, speed with justice, and visibility with inclusion. As AI-enabled finance expands into the Global South, it is exposing an uncomfortable contradiction: the very tools that claim to democratise wealth are often built on infrastructures and assumptions that entrench division. This is the paradox we must confront—before optimism becomes complicity.

At the surface level, AI appears to be closing gaps. Mobile lending apps in Kenya, micro-investment platforms in Indonesia, and robo-advisors targeting gig workers in the Philippines all point to a broader trend: individuals previously shut out of formal financial ecosystems are gaining entry through their phones. The numbers are compelling. M-Pesa, the mobile money platform born in Kenya, enabled over 90% of adults in the country to transact, save, and borrow within a decade of its launch. Startups like Tala, JUMO, and Branch use AI models to assess risk based on smartphone usage, text metadata, and digital footprints—offering credit to those without formal banking histories. In Southeast Asia, apps like Ajaib (Indonesia) and GCash (Philippines) combine sleek UX with machine learning to nudge users toward savings, insurance, and equity investing.

But the story becomes more complex upon closer inspection. What AI grants in accessibility, it often subtracts in agency. Consider the case of algorithmic lending in East Africa. While microloans are disbursed within minutes and require no paperwork, the interest rates are rarely transparent. Borrowers are frequently unaware of how their creditworthiness is calculated—an opacity that prevents recourse or correction. Worse, defaulting on one platform can quietly blacklist a user across others through shared metadata, creating a digital stain with no formal appeal process. The illusion of inclusion masks a system that is structurally extractive: credit is extended not because trust is earned, but because risk is atomised, priced, and absorbed into a model optimised for volume. *Efficiency can be exclusion by another name.*

The inequality paradox also lies in the architecture of the algorithms themselves. Most AI systems are trained on data drawn from digitally saturated environments—users with smartphones, stable internet, predictable usage patterns, and traceable economic activity. These assumptions don't hold in vast swaths of Sub-Saharan Africa or rural Southeast Asia. In these regions, income is irregular, transactions are cash-based, and devices are shared within households. AI trained on urban behaviour may misread such users as unreliable or risky—not because they are, but because the model lacks the cultural calibration to see beyond digital silence. As a result, entire populations are either underserved or mis-served by systems that claim neutrality but encode bias in every line of code.

Moreover, inclusion without education often creates new dependencies. In the Philippines, where digital wallets and stock trading apps have proliferated in recent years, many young users enter financial markets with little understanding of volatility, compounding, or risk diversification. AI-driven platforms nudge them with gamified interfaces, streak rewards, and portfolio "health scores"—mechanisms that feel empowering but often encourage overconfidence. When a market downturn hits, the psychological and financial toll is not just a loss of capital—it is a breakdown of trust. And without local advisory support, recovery is slow or absent. *Technology that delivers tools without context can deepen fragility rather than reduce it.*

A different but equally important dynamic plays out in wealthier enclaves of the same regions. Here, AI tools often reinforce privilege. In Jakarta, Manila, Nairobi, and Lagos, the urban elite increasingly use smart investment platforms that offer personalised portfolios, AI-generated tax optimisation, and global market access—benefits once reserved for institutional investors. These users not only have higher bandwidth and better financial literacy, but also generate richer, more "cooperative" data. As a result, the algorithms learn from them more effectively and optimise more accurately in their favour. Meanwhile, rural or lower-income users generate noisier, harder-to-interpret signals—and thus receive poorer recommendations, higher-risk products, or none at all. *The algorithm is meritocratic only in theory; in practice, it rewards those whose data is legible and profitable.*

To compound the issue, many of these platforms are not locally owned. Silicon Valley venture capital, Chinese fintech giants, and regional conglomerates dominate ownership and infrastructure. Their incentives often prioritise user acquisition over long-term impact, and few are regulated with consumer protection in mind. Data sovereignty becomes a secondary concern, and local knowledge is treated as an edge case, not a design principle. Without structural safeguards, even well-intentioned platforms can become pipelines of extractive capital: drawing value from the periphery and concentrating it at the core. *What looks like empowerment on the surface may be quiet dispossession beneath.*

Is there a way to design AI that resists this drift toward inequity? The answer lies not in abandoning the technology, but in rethinking its assumptions. First, models must be trained on diverse datasets that include non-Western behaviours, informal economic patterns, and low-bandwidth contexts. This requires partnerships with local institutions, not just scraping social media or telecom metadata. Second, algorithms must be auditable and explainable—not just to regulators, but to users themselves. A farmer in Uganda deserves to understand why his loan was denied just as much as a banker in London. Third, financial AI must include feedback loops where users can challenge, correct, and contextualise decisions. Trust cannot be engineered through UX alone; it must be earned through participation.

Encouragingly, some organisations are beginning to explore this path. In Ghana, Bloom Impact offers digital financial products to micro-entrepreneurs while embedding education modules that explain credit terms in local languages. In Vietnam, Timo Bank uses behavioural data to customise savings nudges—but ties them to human advisors trained in financial coaching. And in Rwanda, the startup Exuus is building cooperative savings algorithms rooted in traditional "tontine" practices, blending machine learning with cultural form. These models suggest a future where AI does not overwrite financial tradition, but extends it—*a hybrid intelligence that learns with, not just from, the people it serves.*

The bigger lesson is this: inequality in AI-driven finance is not inevitable. It is a design choice—or more precisely, a series of design omissions. When engineers and investors treat emerging market users as edge cases, they build systems that marginalise by default. When platforms prize growth over comprehension, they foster usage without empowerment. And when inclusion is measured in downloads rather than resilience, the tools of access become the instruments of debt.

AI's potential to democratise finance remains real—but realisation requires friction. It demands that technologists slow down, that local voices be embedded at every level of design, and that we resist the lure of frictionless scalability. Financial systems, at their best, do not merely optimise capital flows. They shape dignity, agency, and the sense of possibility in people's lives. The question is not whether AI can serve this vision. It is whether we will build it to.

Chapter 5
The Ethics of Optimisation

The allure of artificial intelligence in finance rests in its promise of a simple creed: optimisation. Faster returns, sharper allocation, slimmer fees. From the clean dashboards of robo-advisors to the opaque machinery of credit scoring, optimisation has become the silent gospel—an unspoken assumption shaping the flow of billions. Yet one must pause and ask: optimisation towards what? For whom? And at what cost? The deeper we weave machine learning into the fabric of financial decision-making, the more these questions refuse to be ignored. AI is not merely a calculator; it is a set of priorities in code. It does not just mirror the world—it remakes it. What is usually presented as a technical challenge is, in truth, a moral one.

For decades, financial guidance stemmed from a compact consensus: balance risk against reward. This principle, codified in portfolio theory, gave rise to funds, indexes, and advisory structures all oriented around maximising wealth. Even the arrival of digital tools did little to unsettle the paradigm. But AI is something else altogether: less calculator, more architect. It anticipates, nudges, and predicts. It does not wait passively for instructions; it suggests, cajoles, even insists. In doing so, it alters the very meaning of "good" advice. Should a robo-advisor counsel higher equity exposure, is it optimising for long-term gain—or cushioning against the panic of a sudden crash? Should it weigh a child's future tuition against the dream of early retirement? Should efficiency be placed above environmental stewardship? These are not questions of mathematics. They are questions of values.

The supposed neutrality of AI is the first great illusion. Defaults—asset mixes, contribution levels, rules for rebalancing—appear impartial, but they are not. They smuggle in assumptions. Behavioural science shows that defaults wield disproportionate power: automatic enrolment in pensions drives participation skyward; when ESG funds are set as the norm, sustainable investing surges. Preferences do not change—the friction does. AI heightens this effect. Once an algorithm notices that users rarely alter defaults, it may treat those defaults as revealed preference, entrenching them further. What begins as a gentle nudge calcifies into quiet instruction. Choice remains in form, but in practice it is hollow.

The stakes sharpen when the systems falter. Consider algorithmic loan underwriting. Several US fintechs, despite stripping out explicit racial markers, systematically rejected minority applicants by relying on proxies—bill payment histories, shopping patterns, even social graphs. Optimisation sought repayment likelihood, not fairness. In Britain, a major robo-advisor landed in hot water after handing out boilerplate portfolios oblivious to users' liquidity needs—urging aggressive long-term allocations on clients with precarious incomes. Technically sound, perhaps; contextually negligent, certainly.

The root of the issue lies in the training data. History is rarely neutral. Marginalised groups have thinner financial buffers, not through lack of prudence but because of entrenched structural barriers. Models that "optimise" on this historical baseline do not just replicate bias—they codify it, granting inequity the veneer of inevitability. To optimise without interrogating the data's moral freight is intellectual sloth, and when deployed at scale, it becomes institutionalised injustice.

Hence the growing insistence on embedding ethics directly into the optimisation process. One approach is to widen the metrics. Why should a portfolio be judged solely by its Sharpe ratio? Why not also by its carbon footprint, or the gender diversity of the firms it holds? ESG algorithms have attempted this, with mixed success. Too often they lean on flimsy self-reporting or arbitrary scoring, creating the gloss of virtue without its substance. Still, the pivot is telling: from efficiency alone, to efficiency *and.* More promising are value-sensitive platforms that allow users to choose their ethical compass—Shariah-compliant portfolios, carbon-neutral funds, community bonds. Here, optimisation is tuned not just to financial profiles but to moral commitments. The machine becomes translator as much as technician.

Yet values conflict. Should an algorithm favour local employment over global carbon reduction? Divest from tobacco if the company also bankrolls vaccines? Ethical optimisation is not scalar—it resists neat calculation. This throws us back on governance. Who chooses when the user remains silent? How transparent should those choices be? Some answers lie in open-source or decentralised protocols, where optimisation logic can be inspected, forked, challenged. But transparency without literacy risks tokenism; the power is shared only if people can wield it. The future of ethical optimisation thus hinges not merely on algorithms, but on access to the very epistemic tools that interpret them.

Philosophically, this requires us to redefine what it means to "succeed" in finance. If AI is charged with shaping the future, we must first ask: what future do we desire? For some, it is legacy—the passing on of stability. For others, liberation—financial freedom to live differently. Increasingly, especially among younger investors, priorities expand to include sustainability, wellbeing, social impact. These goals are less easily reduced to a metric, but no less real. What once resembled a numbers game is now, unmistakably, a negotiation of values. AI can participate in that conversation—but only if its optimisation goals are intelligible, disputable, and adjustable.

This changes the advisor's role. Far from being supplanted, human advisors are recast as interpreters of ethics and anchors of trust. Their task is to translate the outputs of algorithms into language that resonates, to challenge defaults, to help clients articulate what they value most. The ideal advisor of the future may be less a mathematician than a moral philosopher, equally fluent in compound interest and in questions of meaning.

At the institutional scale, regulators face a parallel task. If AI is to pervade financial life, transparency, explainability, and consent must be hardwired. This means mandating disclosures not just of performance but of objectives. It means auditing models for disparate impact, not merely predictive sharpness. It means funding inquiry into alternative metrics—resilience, dignity, joy, communal stability. These may sound airy, but they are edging into measurable terrain through interdisciplinary collaboration.

Optimisation, then, is not a sterile technicality. It is a cultural statement. Every algorithm carries an implicit answer to the old question: what matters most? To leave that answer unscrutinised is to risk constructing a financial order that grows more potent but less humane. The moment calls for a pause—a refusal to rush past the deeper questions. AI can guide us towards futures. But only we can decide which futures are worthy of pursuit.

What Should AI Optimise For?

Ask a typical financial algorithm what matters most, and the answer will be disarmingly consistent: maximise return, minimise risk. This elegant logic, inherited from decades of economic orthodoxy, remains the beating heart of portfolio theory, automated trading, and most AI-driven advisory systems. It's clean, quantifiable, and has the weight of tradition behind it. But increasingly, it is also inadequate. As artificial intelligence moves from the trading floor to the apps in our pockets and the systems that guide household financial choices, a more complex question emerges—*what should we actually be optimising for?* Because when you ask that question not of a machine, but of a person, the answer is rarely as sterile as "yield". It might be security, time with family, environmental responsibility, or the dignity of leaving behind a legacy. Financial optimisation, once a technical problem, is becoming a deeply human one.

AI systems are only as values-neutral as the metrics they are trained to maximise. The dominance of return as a central metric isn't a feature of financial truth—it's a design decision. A design, crucially, rooted in a narrow conception of human flourishing: that more money equals better outcomes. In some cases, this is fair. But in a world where environmental collapse, mental health crises, and growing inequality undermine the very quality of life that wealth is meant to secure, the assumption begins to fray. *Should the AI managing your pension prioritise raw growth, even if that growth comes from fossil fuels or exploitative labour practices?* Or should it factor in broader criteria—even if that means a slightly lower return?

This is not a hypothetical question. ESG (Environmental, Social, and Governance) investing has exploded over the past decade, and many robo-advisory platforms now offer "sustainable" portfolios. Yet the application of ESG within AI models often amounts to a box-ticking exercise—overlaying traditional asset allocation with lightly filtered indexes based on ratings that lack transparency or consistency. The algorithms still optimise for return; ESG becomes a flavour, not a foundation. The deeper challenge is to reprogramme the AI's core objective function—to embed ethical, psychological, and cultural dimensions into the mathematical logic of optimisation. *Not as afterthoughts, but as first principles.*

Take the example of legacy. For many individuals—especially those later in life—financial decision-making is not about consumption, but continuity. They are less concerned with compounding returns than with transferring values and security to the next generation. Yet few algorithms optimise for intergenerational goals. Even fewer can model the nuanced trade-offs between preserving capital and enabling joy in the present. The language of inheritance—cultural, emotional, and financial—is largely illegible to machine learning systems unless it is quantified. *This points to a deeper tension: AI thrives on numbers, but most of what matters to us isn't numerical.* Meaning, purpose, security—these are not easily graphed.

But nor are they inaccessible. Some platforms are beginning to integrate alternative metrics of wellbeing into financial planning. Consider the rise of "life-centred planning", a framework that asks clients not just about risk appetite but about life satisfaction, community belonging, and time-use priorities. AI, when properly trained, can incorporate this data into adaptive models that recommend not just portfolios but pathways. Should the client reduce working hours to care for a parent? Should they delay retirement to fund a sabbatical for creative work? These decisions do not maximise wealth. They optimise life. The algorithm becomes not a fund selector, but a values-based co-pilot.

Still, there is resistance. The financial industry, steeped in tradition and liability-consciousness, prefers measurable, auditable outcomes. Optimising for sustainability, joy, or fulfilment feels uncomfortably subjective—harder to defend, harder to standardise. But that doesn't mean it's impossible. It means we need new tools. Subjective wellbeing indexes, ecological impact scores, and even psycho-social diagnostics are already being explored by interdisciplinary teams of economists, behavioural scientists, and data ethicists. The question is whether the financial AI sector will have the courage to adopt them—or whether it will continue to optimise for the wrong thing, more efficiently.

Crucially, even within the traditional remit of financial returns, the question of *how* we optimise matters. Maximisation implies linearity: more is always better. But real human preferences are often threshold-based. Someone might want enough to retire early—not infinite compound growth. Another might seek stability over scale, especially after a traumatic financial loss. If AI systems could model *satisficing*—optimising just enough to meet personal thresholds—they could better align with real-world priorities. Yet most current architectures push towards perpetual growth. This has both personal and planetary consequences. On an individual level, it fuels anxiety and overwork. On a global scale, it incentivises extractive investment strategies. *An AI trained only to maximise return will never ask whether that return is desirable, sustainable, or just.*

We must also consider cultural variance. In the United States, financial success is often equated with entrepreneurial risk and visible consumption. In Japan, thrift and long-term planning dominate. Islamic finance adheres to principles of risk-sharing and interest avoidance. In parts of sub-Saharan Africa, wealth is often viewed communally, rather than individually. Optimisation goals in financial AI need to reflect these cultural norms—or risk imposing a monolithic economic logic on diverse human contexts. This is especially urgent as financial platforms scale globally. The same algorithmic architecture that nudges a mid-career American towards aggressive equity exposure may feel alien—or inappropriate—to a risk-averse Malaysian retiree.

A growing field of "ethical AI" in finance is beginning to respond. Projects like FaithFi (which builds Shariah-compliant investing algorithms), Nia Impact Capital (which centres feminist economics), and open-source initiatives like RethinkX's policy simulations aim to reframe what it means to optimise in the first place. These efforts suggest that optimisation is not a fixed endpoint, but a moving target—one that should be co-defined with users, not imposed by coders. *This is the crux: AI should not be deciding what to optimise for. It should be enabling people to decide more clearly for themselves.*

This reframing has deep implications for trust. If users sense that a financial AI serves only market logic, they will view it as extractive or indifferent. But if it transparently aligns with their stated priorities—be they ecological, spiritual, familial, or psychological—it can become a trusted companion. This shift also redefines the role of human advisors. No longer mere explainers of technical products, they become facilitators of ethical clarity—helping clients surface their true goals, weigh competing values, and translate them into actionable frameworks that AI can understand. *It is not optimisation versus ethics. It is optimisation through ethics.*

To design such systems, interdisciplinary literacy is essential. Financial engineers must collaborate with ethicists, anthropologists, and mental health professionals. Regulators must demand explainability not just of how an algorithm works, but of what it aims to achieve. Users must be empowered to choose their optimisation criteria, and to revise them as life evolves. And technologists must build platforms that embrace pluralism, not flatten it.

The future of financial AI will be shaped not by how well it predicts the market, but by how wisely it interprets human goals. In doing so, it must recognise that return on investment is a means, not an end. The real dividends are measured not in basis points, but in freedom, dignity, purpose, and care. As we hand more of our financial decision-making to machines, we are not just outsourcing calculations—we are encoding values. And the question of what to optimise for will define not only our portfolios, but our lives.

The Tyranny of the Default

The most powerful decision you make in a digital system may be the one you don't realise you've made at all. Defaults—those pre-set options presented as the norm in financial interfaces and AI-driven platforms—shape user behaviour with quiet authority. They do not demand attention. They assume it. And therein lies their potency. In the architecture of automated finance, defaults are not just conveniences—they are instructions, encoded choices masquerading as neutrality. When an AI-powered savings app suggests a contribution level, or a robo-advisor preselects an investment mix, or a digital wallet sets a spending alert threshold, the user is nudged not by argument, but by architecture. *And architecture is never neutral.*

Research from behavioural economics has long confirmed the disproportionate impact of defaults. Opt-in versus opt-out structures in retirement savings schemes, for instance, have shown enrolment rates swing from under 50% to over 90% based solely on default framing. When defaults are powered by AI—adapting, learning, and updating based on granular personal data—their influence compounds. These systems don't just recommend; they evolve with you. But they also evolve *for* you, often without sufficient transparency. And as AI becomes the default engine of financial decision-making, the stakes escalate.

Consider a hypothetical, but increasingly typical, scenario. A 28-year-old freelancer signs up for a digital wealth platform. During onboarding, she selects her risk tolerance as "moderate" and time horizon as "long-term". Based on a model trained on millions of similar users, the platform auto-populates a portfolio with 75% equities, 20% bonds, and 5% crypto. She accepts. After all, it looks professional. Later, the platform increases her monthly contribution amount by 10%, citing "progress toward goals". She clicks "approve" again. Eventually, she notices she has little liquidity and high exposure to volatile assets—hardly ideal during a freelance income drought. At no point did she feel forced. But at every point, her behaviour was steered—subtly, smoothly, systematically—by defaults that carried the implicit authority of intelligence. *Was she advised, or was she directed?*

Defaults are not inherently malicious. Often, they are designed with helpful intent—to automate inertia, to protect users from cognitive overload, to increase uptake of beneficial habits. But when defaults are established by systems whose incentives are opaque—or whose optimisations are misaligned with user values—they risk becoming coercive. The line between assistance and manipulation is not demarcated by malice. It is drawn at transparency and consent.

AI complicates this further. In legacy systems, defaults were static: a fixed retirement fund, a standard fee tier, a default bank account link. With AI, defaults become *dynamic*. They are tailored in real-time, adjusting to patterns in your spending, sentiment, and online behaviour. The same interface might present different options to different users—not because one is better, but because one is more *predictively compliant.* This raises sharp ethical questions. If a platform knows that User A is less likely to opt out of higher fees than User B, and it algorithmically sets that as her default, is that intelligence or exploitation? The answer depends not on the algorithm's accuracy, but on its purpose—and its disclosure.

Much of the financial AI ecosystem still operates within what could be called *dark pattern economics*—an approach where system designers understand behavioural bias but use it to serve platform interests rather than user autonomy. Auto-renewals, vague fee structures, and asymmetrical opt-out flows persist even in "transparent" fintech environments. When powered by AI, these patterns scale with unsettling efficiency. A poorly set default is one thing. A self-adjusting, persuasion-optimised default is another entirely.

The downstream effects of defaults are particularly acute in marginalised communities. In regions where financial literacy is uneven—or where users are newly banked through mobile fintech apps—the default carries even greater psychological weight. In parts of Sub-Saharan Africa, for instance, microcredit platforms have been lauded for democratising access. But some of these platforms auto-assign repayment plans or loan sizes based on behaviour inferred by AI from smartphone usage—texts, call logs, location patterns. When these defaults lead to over-indebtedness or missed payments, the user is blamed for non-compliance with a system they never truly understood. *The default becomes destiny.*

Moreover, AI defaults are often shaped not just by internal logic, but by external partnerships. A robo-advisor may default users into funds with higher commissions, not because they are superior, but because they benefit the platform's revenue model. This introduces structural conflict. Optimising for user outcome and optimising for corporate outcome are not always aligned. Without robust disclosure, the user assumes the default is the "best" option—when it may simply be the most profitable one for someone else.

Regulation, where it exists, lags behind practice. Consumer protection bodies in the EU and US have begun examining algorithmic nudging, but most current rules were written for static websites and call centres—not adaptive financial intelligence. In the meantime, it is left to designers, developers, and ethicists within firms to advocate for defaults that are *educative*, not prescriptive. A strong default doesn't just suggest a path. It explains why that path is being suggested, offers viable alternatives, and makes deviation easy. It assumes agency, not passivity.

Designers of financial AI must also consider default effects in emotionally charged moments. During economic shocks, illness, divorce, or death, users are particularly vulnerable. Defaults that lock users into low-liquidity positions or risky allocations during such times may satisfy an optimisation function, but violate a moral one. Systems must be calibrated not just to maximise resilience, but to recognise fragility.

There are signs of progress. A handful of firms now offer *default transparency protocols*—where users are shown how their default options were derived, which variables were weighted, and how to adjust them. Others use *reverse defaults*, where the user begins with a blank slate and is gradually shown options, ranked by trade-offs rather than predicted compliance. Such approaches encourage reflection rather than reaction. They frame AI not as a silent puppet-master, but as a conversational partner.

Importantly, the concept of the "default" should not be limited to user interface settings. In AI financial systems, default logic is embedded in training data, in model architectures, in assumptions about goals. If the model is trained on historical data where certain groups were denied credit more often, its predictions will default to replicating that exclusion. If a wealth management AI assumes retirement at 65 as a default goal, it may under-serve gig workers, artists, or early retirees. *To interrogate the default is to interrogate the foundation of the machine itself.*

At its most profound, the tyranny of the default is not about buttons or toggles. It's about epistemology—*who decides what is "normal" in financial life, and why?* When defaults become invisible norms, they shape not just our decisions, but our definitions of success, security, and sufficiency. The default, then, is not just a design choice. It is a moral stance.

The future of ethical AI in finance will depend not just on more powerful models, but on more thoughtful defaults. Defaults that invite curiosity. Defaults that disclose bias. Defaults that recede when autonomy asserts itself. And above all, defaults that respect the complexity of human life—a life that no machine, no matter how intelligent, should ever presume to predefine.

When Good Advice Goes Wrong

The most dangerous financial advice is not the advice that's obviously bad. It's the kind that looks good, sounds rational, passes every statistical check—but fails to account for the complexity of real lives. In the age of artificial intelligence, this risk takes on a new dimension. Automated systems increasingly mediate how people save, invest, borrow, and plan. When those systems offer guidance, it arrives with an aura of precision, backed by machine learning models trained on vast datasets. The outputs seem unimpeachable. But when these outputs fail—subtly or spectacularly—the fallout can be deeply personal and profoundly unfair.

One of the most visible failures of AI-driven financial advice lies in the realm of credit scoring. Several high-profile investigations, including a 2019 case involving Apple Card's underwriting algorithms, exposed how women—despite equivalent credit profiles—received significantly lower credit limits than men. The culprit wasn't explicit programming bias, but historical data and opaque correlations embedded in the training sets. These systems didn't intend to discriminate. But *intent is irrelevant when impact is systemic*. When algorithms inherit bias, they scale it. Worse, they disguise it beneath the veneer of objectivity.

The myth of algorithmic neutrality often masks the real issue: optimisation divorced from context. An AI system may learn that certain zip codes, spending behaviours, or income patterns correlate with higher default rates. It will act on these correlations, not because it understands causation, but because they optimise predictive accuracy. But what if the data reflects decades of discriminatory lending practices or underinvestment in certain communities? In such cases, *good advice becomes complicit in perpetuating harm*. A borrower is declined not because they are unworthy, but because their profile echoes a history of being overlooked.

The problem extends beyond credit. Many fintech savings tools, especially those built for low- to moderate-income users, encourage automated saving based on "safe-to-save" algorithms. These systems scan a user's income and spending patterns, then move small amounts of money into savings accounts or investment platforms. On the surface, this looks empowering. Users save without thinking, building healthy habits through automation. But for those living close to the margin, even a £10 transfer can trigger overdraft fees, bounced bills, or food insecurity. In several reported instances, users of these apps found themselves financially stranded—*optimised into liquidity traps by systems that mistook stability for surplus.*

What these cases reveal is not the malevolence of technology, but the blind spots of design. Many financial AI systems are built by data scientists, engineers, and product managers who have never lived paycheque to paycheque, navigated structural inequality, or juggled financial responsibilities across multiple family members and currencies. The algorithms they design often embody implicit assumptions about what "normal" financial behaviour looks like: regular income, predictable expenses, rational trade-offs. But for many users—gig workers, single parents, migrants, informal entrepreneurs—normal is anything but stable. A system optimised on standard inputs can be dangerously misaligned with atypical but entirely valid financial realities.

Even well-funded robo-advisors fall prey to this misalignment. Consider the case of emergency savings. Traditional financial planning advice recommends maintaining three to six months of living expenses in an accessible account before investing aggressively. Yet many robo-advisors, particularly in their early iterations, skipped this step. They encouraged users to invest recurring contributions straight into market-tracking ETFs, maximising long-term returns. For users who later faced job losses, medical emergencies, or sudden relocations, this meant liquidating assets at a loss—sometimes incurring tax penalties or missing recovery windows. *The algorithm optimised for the average outcome, not the real-time risk.*

This speaks to a deeper philosophical tension: should financial AI optimise for precision or resilience? A model may be 92% accurate on average, but if the 8% of edge cases represent real, vulnerable people, then average accuracy is a poor ethical defence. The same logic applies to retirement planning tools. Several digital platforms have pushed users toward delayed retirement dates, assuming longevity and stable employment. But for users facing burnout, age discrimination, or chronic illness, such projections border on fiction. Systems that fail to ask *whether* a user wants to work until 70, or *whether* they can, are not giving advice—they're issuing verdicts.

The problem is compounded when users lack the literacy or confidence to question algorithmic outputs. In traditional human advising, a client can ask "Why?" and receive a nuanced answer. With AI, the logic is often inaccessible, hidden behind black-box models or summarised in generic tooltips. When advice goes wrong, there is no one to call. No feedback loop. No empathy. Just a static dashboard insisting that your risk score, your budget, your goals, make sense—even when they don't.

A case study from Southeast Asia highlights the fragility of this model. A digital lending app, targeting underbanked populations in Indonesia and the Philippines, used smartphone metadata—like battery levels, typing speed, and contact lists—to assess creditworthiness. For many first-time borrowers, this was their only option. But when defaults occurred, some platforms began sending debt reminders not just to the borrowers but to their contacts—friends, family, even employers—triggering public shame and reputational damage. The algorithm had "learned" that social pressure reduced delinquency. *What it hadn't learned was the human cost of that strategy.*

These failures expose a critical truth: advice cannot be reduced to output. Good advice involves context, discretion, values, and dialogue. AI can model patterns. It can simulate scenarios. But it cannot yet *understand* the emotional, cultural, and circumstantial nuances that make financial life so irreducibly human. And when it tries to do so without proper guardrails, oversight, or ethical frameworks, it can cause quiet harm at scale.

There is a way forward, but it requires a rethinking of what "smart" means in financial technology. Smart doesn't mean maximally optimised. It means adaptive, transparent, accountable, and pluralistic. Smart advice doesn't assume the same goal for every user. It asks what matters to *this* person—security, freedom, family, status, philanthropy—and adjusts accordingly. This demands the inclusion of social workers, psychologists, ethicists, and user advocates in the design of financial AI—not just quants and coders.

Some platforms are beginning to experiment with "explainable advice"—where each recommendation is accompanied by plain-language justifications, confidence levels, and scenario alternatives. Others are integrating human support layers: trained financial coaches who can intervene when the model flags uncertainty or detects unusual patterns. A few are exploring *consent architecture*—allowing users to toggle their optimisation preferences between "growth", "security", "flexibility", or "community contribution". These are not fixes. But they are steps toward advice that is not just smart, but wise.

The pathologies of AI-guided finance do not lie in the technology itself. They lie in what we choose to optimise, who we empower to define success, and how we design for failure. Financial advice, at its best, is a form of care. It helps people articulate their values, navigate trade-offs, and prepare for the unknown. When AI fails to do this, it doesn't just offer bad advice. *It forgets what advice is for.*

To avoid these failures, we must resist the seduction of certainty. The best financial systems will not eliminate ambiguity—they will help users engage with it. They will honour the unpredictability of life, the multiplicity of goals, and the necessity of grace. That is the promise of truly intelligent finance: not perfection, but perspective. Not control, but compassion. And not just advice that computes, but advice that understands.

Values in the Machine

A financial algorithm does not have a soul. It doesn't pray. It doesn't protest. It does not weigh the suffering of a garment worker against the quarterly returns of a multinational textile fund. Yet, paradoxically, this soul-less machine is now responsible for allocating trillions of dollars in capital around the world—guiding pensions, retirement portfolios, sovereign wealth funds, and even the philanthropic distributions of impact investors. The question that demands our attention is no longer whether artificial intelligence should be used to shape financial decision-making—it already is. The question is whether that intelligence can be aligned with human values.

Historically, financial optimisation has been synonymous with return maximisation. This model treats all dollars equally, regardless of how they were earned or what they finance. A tobacco conglomerate and a renewable energy startup are judged by the same metrics: projected growth, risk-adjusted yield, volatility. The machine doesn't care who gets hurt. But people do. And as more capital flows through autonomous systems—recommendation engines, robo-advisors, portfolio constructors—an urgent movement has emerged: to encode ethics into financial AI. To teach the machine not just to think, but to *care*.

The most visible expression of this effort is the rise of ESG AI—artificial intelligence tools trained to integrate environmental, social, and governance (ESG) considerations into investment decisions. These systems scrape vast troves of unstructured data—from climate reports to labour violations to board diversity disclosures—and produce ESG ratings or risk flags that guide capital away from harmful companies and toward more sustainable ones. The ambition is noble. But the execution is deeply contested.

Consider two AI models assessing the same oil company. One model, trained by a risk-focused asset manager, may rate the company highly for having robust climate disclosures and transitioning towards biofuels. Another, trained by a climate justice NGO, may penalise the same firm for legacy pollution, lobbying efforts, or continued exploration in sensitive regions. Both use AI. Both cite "sustainability." But they optimise for fundamentally different values. This is not a technical problem—it is a philosophical one. *The neutrality of the algorithm is a myth; values are embedded from the start.*

Faith-aligned investing algorithms take this tension further. In the past, faith-based portfolios—Islamic, Christian, Jewish—were curated manually, excluding sectors like gambling, alcohol, or weapons. Today, AI models can automate this filtering at scale, parsing financial statements, vendor relationships, and product catalogues to flag companies in breach of ethical guidelines derived from religious texts or moral doctrines. For example, Islamic fintech platforms are building sharia-compliant robo-advisors that exclude interest-bearing instruments and invest in businesses aligned with halal principles. This isn't fringe experimentation—it's a billion-dollar innovation grounded in centuries of jurisprudence. *What emerges is a financial system that is not just efficient, but spiritually legible.*

But values embedded in machines also create new dilemmas. Who decides what counts as "ethical"? What happens when values collide—when an ESG fund includes a solar panel manufacturer that relies on forced labour in Xinjiang? Or when a faith-based screen excludes a company for ideological reasons but the user prioritises economic empowerment for marginalised communities? AI does not resolve these tensions; it makes them more urgent. And unless these models are transparent—unless users can interrogate the logic behind their outputs—trust will erode.

Transparency alone, however, is not sufficient. The financial industry is now grappling with the need for *open-source planning models*—systems where not just the outputs, but the logic, datasets, and assumptions behind AI tools are open to audit, critique, and improvement. A handful of initiatives, like OpenAI for ESG or community-governed planning frameworks in Latin America, are pioneering these structures. By decentralising governance and embedding public values into model architecture, they aim to produce financial intelligence that is democratically accountable. These efforts remain nascent, but they gesture towards a future in which *AI is not just a tool of capital, but a custodian of conscience.*

Still, the problem runs deeper than disclosure or modular ethics. Most AI systems are trained on historical data. That data encodes the past: a world of inequity, extraction, and exclusion. When AI learns from that past without critical override, it risks perpetuating it. A portfolio optimiser trained on decades of market performance might, for example, favour fossil fuels over green energy because the former delivered steadier returns. Unless explicitly reprogrammed to prioritise sustainability—even at the cost of returns—the system will replicate yesterday's logic. In this way, *a purely backward-looking AI becomes a barrier to progress.*

The solution is not to pretend AI can be value-neutral. The solution is to *own the values*, declare them, debate them, and build systems that can flex across worldviews. A pluralistic financial AI ecosystem might offer users the ability to toggle their investment priorities across multiple axes: environmental resilience, human rights, religious compliance, intergenerational equity. These priorities would then feed into the recommendation engine, allowing for bespoke advice that reflects not just the client's risk tolerance, but their moral imagination. *Advice, after all, is never just about what we can afford—it's about who we want to be.*

One promising direction is the integration of stakeholder perspectives during model development. A growing number of fintech firms are convening panels composed of climate scientists, ethicists, theologians, Indigenous leaders, and community organisers to help define model parameters. These aren't token exercises. In some cases, their insights have directly reshaped algorithms—prompting exclusions of firms complicit in ecological degradation or prompting the inclusion of community-owned cooperatives. *Embedding ethics into AI is not just about software; it's about sovereignty—who gets to shape the future of finance.*

Even the very definition of optimisation is up for debate. Should a wealth planner optimise for intergenerational legacy, or for personal happiness? For income smoothing, or for carbon reduction? Some platforms now allow users to state their "life goals" alongside their financial goals—prompting the system to recommend investments, savings plans, or donations aligned with qualitative aspirations. A user might prioritise local economic development over short-term growth. Another might aim for financial independence while minimising social harm. These models treat capital not as an end, but as a means—to agency, to purpose, to justice.

There are no perfect models. Values conflict. Trade-offs are inevitable. But if we pretend that financial AI is a neutral oracle, we surrender control of our moral agency. The task before us is not to eliminate value judgments from AI. It is to *surface them*, structure them, and make them intelligible to users. We need financial systems that ask not only *what is likely to grow*, but also *what is worth growing.*

In the end, the movement to embed values into the machine is not a rejection of technology—it is an insistence that *intelligence must serve integrity*. The future of finance will be shaped not just by what we optimise, but by what we reimagine. And in that reimagining lies the opportunity to build systems that are not only smart, but just. Not only efficient, but ethical. Not only autonomous, but aligned—with the messy, beautiful, contradictory values that make us human.

Chapter 6
Children of the Algorithm

For much of human history, wealth travelled in a straight line. Property, coin, land—passed hand to hand, carried forward through paper deeds, family agreements, and the authority of courts. Legacy meant wills, signatures, and trusted intermediaries. Now, that order is fraying. As artificial intelligence seeps into the structures of finance, inheritance is less about static ledgers and more about dynamic architectures. Wealth is not merely stored; it is modelled, interpreted, even adapted. AI does not simply preserve what we leave—it begins to participate in defining what it means.

What was once a financial estate—lists of assets, liabilities, and succession clauses—has begun to mutate into something more fluid: a living digital framework. Alongside the numbers arrive annotations, scenarios, predictive logic. Inheritance, once transactional, now edges toward dialogue. It is as though the dead continue to speak, not through a single will but through systems that can anticipate, test, and refine intentions across time.

This is not speculative. It is already taking form. Legal-tech firms now deploy smart contracts that execute estate instructions automatically upon verified events. "Dynamic wills" adapt themselves as conditions shift—a new child born, markets lurching, health altering probabilities. Predictive models simulate outcomes, showing families how different distributions might play out across decades. Old tools laid down rules; new ones explore reasons.

But convenience is only the surface. By embedding intentions in programmable form, families begin to code values into their legacies. A parent may, for instance, stipulate that funds for education be released only if a grandchild pursues work aligned with sustainability. Once awkward or impossible to enforce, such clauses are now within reach. Yet this raises uncomfortable questions: is it an authentic expression of legacy, or a subtle exertion of control? At what point does wisdom harden into coercion?

The rise of "crypto-vaults" makes this even starker. Digital natives hold not just currency but tokens, NFTs, parcels of digital real estate, and algorithmic assets. These require infrastructures—secure multi-signature systems, biometric triggers, or consensus-based transfers. Services like Casa and TrustVerse already build such frameworks. Yet the key is literacy. A recovery phrase might unlock millions, but only if heirs know what it is, how to wield it, and what dangers lie around it.

Here education shifts dramatically. Teaching the next generation to manage wealth will not end with compound interest charts or household budgeting. It will demand fluency in data structures, algorithmic assumptions, and probabilistic models. Heirs will need to spot biases, understand how systems draw inferences, and challenge the frameworks shaping their choices. In other words, wealth stewardship becomes less about thrift and more about interpretive agility.

Some families are already experimenting. Static documents give way to narrative archives—blends of financial logs, ethical reflections, and family philosophies. AI lends itself curiously well here. Large language models can help elders capture not just their balance sheets, but their convictions. Instead of a single line allocating ten per cent to charity, a living archive may explain why, illustrate impact, even invite revision from descendants. Others have gone further, training "ancestor bots" on diaries, recordings, and correspondence, creating digital presences that can be consulted long after the body is gone.

The idea is poignant—and troubling. At what point does remembrance collapse into simulation? Can a machine proxy genuinely guide a teenager in a world the ancestor never imagined? Or is it merely a digitised echo, risking nostalgia over imagination? What happens when we inherit not only assets, but fragments of cognition?

All this reframes what we mean by literacy. To inherit in the age of AI is to recognise the biases embedded in code: the North American assumptions baked into "global" models, the risk profiles drawn from male behavioural data, the ESG scores dependent on Western disclosure regimes. An heir who takes AI's recommendations at face value may inherit not only wealth, but the prejudices of the data that trained it. The responsible heir must learn to interrogate, to adjust, to resist.

This, in turn, forces reflection on what legacies matter. Money is only part of it. Cultural, social, and moral inheritances may carry equal weight. AI platforms are increasingly able to fold these into financial architectures—measuring impact, aligning portfolios with collective missions, or simulating outcomes of moral commitments. Families might allocate wealth not strictly by blood, but by contribution to shared goals, or by alignment with communal values. These practices are not hypothetical; they are being trialled already by philanthropic networks that view wealth as stewardship rather than entitlement.

And yet—AI cannot carry the emotional burden. It may streamline the paperwork, simulate the trade-offs, or translate intentions into executable code. But it cannot dissolve love, rivalry, disappointment, or forgiveness. Nor should it. If anything, its increasing sophistication underlines the irreplaceable role of human choice. The wisest planning is not AI-led but AI-informed. Machines illuminate; people decide.

So we are left with a broader inquiry: how does intelligence, artificial or otherwise, intersect with legacy? What does it mean to embed not just capital, but memory and intention, into systems that may outlast us? This is no mere technical debate; it is a cultural reckoning.

As wealth grows more digitised, more distributed, the central question shifts. It is no longer simply: *how shall we pass it on?* It becomes: *what deserves to be passed at all?* The answer will not lie in code. It will lie in the values we choose to encode. Whether our descendants inherit tools for freedom or scaffolds of control will depend not on the ingenuity of the algorithms, but on the clarity of our own vision of legacy.

AI and Intergenerational Wealth

What we leave behind has always been a mirror of what we value. Yet in the age of artificial intelligence, legacy is no longer a static transfer of property—it is becoming a dynamic interface between generations, one shaped as much by algorithms as by intention. For families navigating the future of wealth, AI is not simply a planning tool; it is a force capable of shaping what the next generation will consider valuable, ethical, and even meaningful. *When software becomes part of the inheritance, it does more than organise the estate—it redefines it.*

The core promise of AI in legacy planning lies in its capacity to manage complexity with unprecedented precision. Estate structures that once demanded teams of accountants and legal advisors can now be coordinated through intelligent systems capable of modelling future scenarios, tax implications, and distribution strategies at scale. AI-driven platforms like Vanilla and Trust & Will in the United States, or Everplans and Farewill in the UK, are beginning to automate not only document generation but the adaptive modelling of family needs over time. These platforms draw on both static data—like net worth and asset classes—and dynamic signals such as health status, market conditions, or regulatory changes. The result is a shift from static planning to *living strategy*, where the concept of a "final" will becomes obsolete.

But capability is not the same as wisdom. The deeper question is not whether AI can optimise inheritance—it already can—but *what* it chooses to optimise for, and what values it encodes along the way. Consider the growing trend of algorithmically defined wealth triggers: clauses that release funds only upon certain behaviours, like graduating university or starting a business. These logic-based instructions, once the preserve of elaborate trusts for the ultra-wealthy, are now increasingly available through mid-market digital estate tools. The mechanism is efficient. The implication is profound. *We are now encoding behavioural expectations into machines that will outlive us.* In doing so, we risk turning legacy into a conditional transaction, rather than a space for growth and autonomy.

AI also introduces new categories of inheritance—assets that have no physical presence, no paper trail, and often no national jurisdiction. From cryptocurrency wallets to digital art, decentralised identities to intellectual property stored in the cloud, the definition of inheritable wealth is expanding faster than most legal frameworks can accommodate. Yet the real challenge is not custodial, but conceptual. A digital asset may be technically transferable, but what if the next generation does not see it as valuable? Or worse, what if the asset requires knowledge of a protocol, a key, or a platform that no longer exists? *Without shared understanding, wealth can become invisible.*

This raises the question: what does financial literacy look like across generations shaped by different tools, different norms, and different ontologies of value? A 60-year-old may view diversified portfolios and passive income as the pinnacle of financial maturity; a 25-year-old might see liquidity in the form of tokenised assets and community-based decentralised finance (DeFi) as the real metric of freedom. AI is increasingly mediating between these worlds—offering both parties translations of wealth through dashboards, scenario engines, and recommendation layers. Yet in mediating, it also interprets. And interpretation is never neutral.

For instance, robo-advisory platforms trained on historical data may subtly reinforce legacy definitions of success: wealth maximisation, tax minimisation, low volatility. But what happens when a young heir wants to weight their portfolio toward climate impact, local regeneration, or social cohesion—metrics that don't fit traditional financial models? Some AI systems will dismiss these as irrational preferences. Others—like those integrated with ESG scoring models or alternative KPIs—will adapt. The distinction is not technical. It is philosophical. *The design of the algorithm reflects the worldview of its creators—and will, in turn, shape the worldview of its users.*

Families are beginning to recognise this, and some are responding by embedding multi-generational dialogue into their planning. Digital storytelling tools such as Storyworth, or family governance platforms like Trusted Family, allow for more than asset transfer: they help capture decision logic, moral reasoning, and family narratives. AI-enhanced versions of these tools can summarise, translate, or even generate intergenerational content—letters to future heirs, annotated life timelines, or interactive legacy archives. These are not just sentimental add-ons. They are interpretive layers that help future custodians understand not only what they've inherited, but *why*.

Still, caution is warranted. Not all families agree on legacy goals—and AI has a tendency to flatten nuance. A system trained to align with family values may overfit to one generation's views while excluding dissenting voices or evolving perspectives. Worse, it may hard-code outdated assumptions under the guise of continuity. *To protect against this, financial AI must be designed with interpretive pluralism in mind*—offering transparency into its logic, and the capacity for human override. In other words, the best algorithms for legacy planning are those that *invite challenge*, not enforce obedience.

AI also introduces a delicate shift in temporality. Traditional estate planning looks backwards: it accounts for what has been accumulated. AI-inflected planning, by contrast, is inherently forward-facing. It models futures. It simulates risk trajectories, behavioural outcomes, and even intergenerational sentiment analysis based on inputs like spending habits, social activity, and value-aligned surveys. The implication is subtle but profound: *we are no longer just planning for our children, we are predicting them.* Whether this helps or harms depends on how such predictions are used. At best, they can offer insight into how to support autonomy and capability. At worst, they risk pathologising deviation from predefined behavioural templates.

Moreover, AI invites a rethinking of what *non-monetary* legacy can mean. Increasingly, families are exploring ways to formalise intellectual, cultural, and ethical inheritance—creating archives of decisions, dilemmas, and belief systems that can be referenced or reinterpreted by descendants. Some are even training personal AI models on their communications, preferences, and digital footprints, creating what amounts to algorithmic avatars. These can respond to questions, simulate advice, or offer synthetic companionship. The aim is not immortality, but *continuity*. Whether this is wise or illusory is still under debate—but its existence is no longer speculative.

What AI makes possible is not simply efficiency, but *intelligibility across generations*. It creates a scaffolding for values, a toolset for stewardship, and a framework in which decisions can be revisited, refined, and, critically, questioned. But that same scaffolding can become a constraint if not designed with humility. The legacy we leave behind must be *legible* to the future—not just as data, but as meaning. This requires anticipating not only financial volatility, but cultural change.

To treat AI as merely a calculator for inheritance is to ignore its deeper role as a cultural force. It does not just organise what we leave; it shapes how we imagine what is worth leaving. In this light, legacy is no longer a set of documents or a fixed corpus of wealth. It is a negotiated, evolving structure—part financial, part narrative, part algorithmic. And its success will depend not on the technical sophistication of our tools, but on the *moral clarity and cultural fluency with which we design them.*

Intergenerational wealth, in the context of AI, becomes less about possession and more about translation—between worldviews, between timelines, between epistemologies of value. The task ahead is not to automate legacy but to humanise it, using machines not as arbiters, but as instruments—intelligent, adaptable, and always in service of a conversation that no algorithm can complete on our behalf.

The Inheritance Interface

The act of inheritance has always been about more than the distribution of assets—it is an expression of continuity, a bridge between generations. Yet the mechanics of inheritance have largely remained analog, governed by legal instruments that struggle to keep pace with the fluidity of wealth in the digital age. Today, as AI-driven systems begin to infiltrate the domain of estate planning, they are not merely digitising the will—they are transforming the interface of legacy itself. What was once handwritten and notarised is now code-based, conditional, adaptive. And while these innovations promise efficiency and access, they also raise critical questions about agency, fairness, and the long-term intelligibility of wealth.

At the centre of this shift is the smart will—a programmable contract that uses blockchain-based infrastructure to automate the execution of inheritance instructions. Unlike traditional wills, which rely on executors and probate courts, smart wills operate on pre-coded logic and distributed consensus. Assets—particularly digital ones like cryptocurrency, NFTs, or tokenised equity—are released upon verification of conditions such as time delays, biometric authentication, or verified life events. The result is a streamlined, theoretically tamper-proof mechanism for asset transfer. But *the elimination of human intermediaries does not eliminate the need for judgment.* In fact, it amplifies the importance of anticipating complexity in the coding of one's final wishes.

This new paradigm extends to crypto-vaults and multi-signature wallets, designed not only to protect digital assets during a holder's lifetime but also to facilitate their seamless transfer across generations. Services like Casa, Safe (formerly Gnosis Safe), and Ledger Enterprise are building infrastructures that allow families to structure access hierarchies, implement time-based rules, and assign recovery rights in decentralised formats. These tools cater especially to those whose wealth exists outside traditional banking systems—a growing demographic of investors, digital entrepreneurs, and global citizens who no longer see borders as relevant to their financial identity. *For them, inheritance is no longer about estate law; it is about key management and smart contract integrity.*

Yet even as digital inheritance infrastructure becomes more sophisticated, it risks becoming more opaque. A smart will may be functionally secure, but if its logic is inscrutable to its beneficiaries—or if the platforms it depends on are deprecated, hacked, or restructured—the wealth it controls may become inaccessible. Moreover, the assumption that all heirs are technically literate or have equal access to these systems is a dangerous one. Without adequate educational scaffolding, automation can produce a veneer of precision while sowing confusion, inequity, or even unresolvable conflict.

AI is stepping into this breach by offering predictive models for family wealth transfer, capable of anticipating financial needs, behavioural responses, and even inter-sibling dynamics. Platforms like Bento Engine and Shaping Wealth are already layering behavioural science and machine learning into wealth advisory tools—allowing parents, for example, to simulate how different inheritance structures might affect their children's financial wellbeing or emotional relationship to money. Some systems go further, modelling optimal distribution timelines to avoid the psychological shock of a large windfall or to incentivise long-term stewardship. But as with all predictive technologies, *the question is not only what the model can forecast—but who decides what counts as an optimal outcome.*

This brings us to a deeper tension embedded in the inheritance interface: *the codification of values.* A will is not simply a financial document; it is a moral artefact. It conveys priorities, affections, boundaries. When translated into code, those messages risk becoming flattened—shorn of context, nuance, and the capacity for reinterpretation. For example, a clause that withholds funds until a beneficiary reaches a certain age may seem prudent. But what if life circumstances require earlier access? Or what if the triggering condition—such as graduating from a particular institution—reflects a bias or assumption that the next generation no longer shares? Codified logic offers no room for mercy, adaptability, or reinterpretation in light of changing realities.

Some families and advisors are responding by integrating narrative and advisory layers into inheritance planning. This includes the creation of digital legacy statements, video wills, or AI-curated repositories of personal reflections. Tools like Eterneva, Life Legacy, or bespoke applications built atop GPT-powered platforms allow users to record and transmit not only instructions but intentions. These digital adjuncts aim to preserve what a purely transactional inheritance cannot: *the story of why certain decisions were made, and how they might be understood over time.* However, this shift from instruction to narrative introduces its own challenges. Who curates the story? Can it be edited? Will it evolve?

A further implication of the inheritance interface is its potential to drive global standardisation of legacy logic. As platforms scale and white-label their services across jurisdictions, there is a risk that local cultural norms, religious traditions, or alternative conceptions of inheritance may be marginalised. In countries where familial wealth transfer follows oral traditions or community-based distributions, the digitisation of inheritance might impose frameworks that undermine communal trust or autonomy. *The interface, in other words, is never neutral. It is a product of its design assumptions—and those assumptions carry cultural weight.*

To counterbalance this, some technologists and legal scholars are calling for the development of open-source inheritance protocols—flexible frameworks that allow for jurisdictional variation, cultural adaptation, and future-proofing. These initiatives echo broader movements in civic technology and digital rights, where the emphasis is on transparency, modifiability, and decentralised governance. While still nascent, such efforts hold promise in ensuring that the inheritance infrastructure of the future is not locked into proprietary systems that outlive their relevance or exploit their users' asymmetrical understanding.

One of the most underappreciated consequences of the new inheritance interface is the temporal decoupling of decision and effect. In the traditional model, a will is activated posthumously and implemented relatively quickly. In the AI-driven model, a digital estate plan may span decades, evolving dynamically as circumstances change. This shift introduces both opportunity and vulnerability. On one hand, *legacy becomes responsive*—able to accommodate life events, market conditions, or personal growth. On the other, it becomes dependent on systems that must themselves remain secure, interpretable, and accessible across time. If those systems fail—technologically, legally, or ethically—the consequences may be felt long after the originator is gone.

Ultimately, the inheritance interface challenges us to reconceive what we mean by legacy. It is no longer sufficient to think of inheritance as a set of legal documents and asset classes. We must also reckon with its digital scaffolding, its behavioural implications, and its encoded philosophies. The tools we use to transmit wealth are shaping the kind of wealth we value, and the values we attach to it. The rise of smart wills, crypto-vaults, and predictive AI in estate planning marks a profound shift—not just in technology, but in the architecture of memory, meaning, and family continuity.

As this architecture matures, the imperative will be to ensure that it remains legible to human beings—not just to machines. That it invites conversation rather than silencing it. That it adapts not only to market dynamics but to the unpredictable contours of real lives. The inheritance interface, if built with care, can become a bridge—not a barrier—between the intentions of one generation and the evolving needs of the next. But to achieve this, it must be designed not only for precision, but for wisdom.

Wealth Education in an AI World –

Financial literacy has long been tethered to the arithmetic of budgeting, the discipline of saving, and the basic understanding of interest, debt, and investing. It was taught through ledgers, worksheets, and later, apps—tools that trained individuals to manage money as a finite commodity. But in the context of artificial intelligence, financial knowledge is undergoing a fundamental shift. Today's youth are not inheriting static rules about compound interest or line-item budgets. They are stepping into a world governed by dynamic systems—ecosystems of intelligent automation, predictive analytics, behavioural nudges, tokenised assets, and algorithmic governance. In this world, understanding *how* systems think matters more than memorising *what* systems do.

This transformation in financial literacy is not merely a matter of technological novelty. It's epistemological. Just as the Industrial Age required a population literate in mechanical systems and the Digital Age demanded fluency in information processing, the AI age requires fluency in *systemic interdependence.* Children now growing up with AI-powered assistants, algorithmic recommendations, and intelligent financial tools must learn to interrogate design, assess systemic incentives, and anticipate feedback loops. They are not being asked simply to balance books. They are being asked to navigate an ever-adapting terrain where automation makes choices *on their behalf*—from which savings goals to prioritise, to which financial behaviours to reward.

This raises profound questions for educators, parents, and policymakers alike: What, exactly, is financial education in a world where systems can "learn" faster than students? Should we be teaching children how to operate calculators, or how to audit algorithms? Is the goal to master spreadsheets—or to cultivate critical reasoning about system defaults, data ethics, and behavioural economics? The stakes are high. Without a systemic mindset, the next generation may become passive consumers of financial automation—trusting outputs without understanding inputs, and misreading convenience as intelligence.

Take, for example, the widespread adoption of robo-advisors and automated financial planning tools. These services, while democratising access to sophisticated modelling, also shield users from the underlying assumptions that drive decisions. A portfolio's risk profile may be optimised by AI, but on what basis? Is it historical volatility, liquidity preferences, age-based heuristics, or inferred behavioural patterns? Few users know, and even fewer challenge it. If children are not taught to question these parameters—much less understand them—then financial literacy becomes financial obedience.

In response, a new pedagogy is emerging—one that views financial literacy not as a checklist of numeracy skills, but as an interdisciplinary fluency that incorporates data ethics, cognitive science, system design, and computational thinking. Rather than starting with concepts like "interest rates" or "budgets," some forward-thinking educators now begin with system mapping exercises: showing how a decision in one domain (say, climate policy) creates ripple effects in another (like insurance costs or commodity prices). These lessons frame finance as a *living system*, not a static silo. From here, students are better prepared to engage with intelligent tools—not just as users, but as informed collaborators.

Practical applications are already surfacing. Some programmes introduce teenagers to algorithmic literacy by letting them experiment with AI-powered budgeting tools in sandbox environments. Others use blockchain simulations to teach the logic of decentralised finance (DeFi), letting students see first-hand how smart contracts govern transactions without central authority. Still others explore "value simulation" games, where players assign weights to competing goals like profit, social justice, and sustainability—forcing them to confront the trade-offs that even the most advanced AI cannot resolve without human direction. These experiences do not teach financial literacy *despite* technology; they teach it *through* and *about* technology.

Cultural context also matters. The idea of financial literacy-as-systems-thinking is not uniformly embraced across nations or education systems. In highly standardised curriculums, such as those in much of Europe, the integration of financial AI is slow, stymied by bureaucratic inertia. In contrast, informal educational ecosystems—such as coding bootcamps, online academies, and gamified learning platforms—are moving more nimbly. Platforms like MyBnk (UK), EverFi (US), and Smart Money Africa (Nigeria) are experimenting with modules that combine behavioural psychology with system-level thinking, helping young people frame financial knowledge not as isolated skills but as an adaptive capacity.

However, this shift is not without its tensions. A system-level approach to financial education inevitably downplays rote memorisation in favour of conceptual understanding—and this requires both pedagogical creativity and curricular freedom. More fundamentally, it demands we accept a discomforting truth: *we cannot teach kids everything they need to know; we must teach them how to keep learning when the system itself evolves.* In an AI-rich world, the half-life of any given financial rule is shrinking. What endures is the learner's ability to frame questions, probe systems, and reason under uncertainty.

There is also the ethical dimension. Teaching children to "understand systems" necessarily invites them to reflect on values. AI systems are not neutral; they encode priorities, incentives, and biases—often invisibly. Financial recommendation engines might favour risk-aversion for some users and risk-taking for others, depending on opaque profiling. Without ethical literacy, students may mistake statistical patterns for moral authority. A system that advises a 16-year-old to invest in fossil fuel ETFs because of historical return rates may technically be "optimal," but is it desirable? Here, financial education must intersect with civics, sustainability, and identity—asking not just *what* AI recommends, but *why* we might accept or reject that recommendation.

Family environments can either reinforce or contradict these learnings. For generations, financial education within households has been framed in anecdotal terms—"save for a rainy day," "never borrow more than you earn," "invest in property." These heuristics, shaped by the economic realities of their time, are not always transferable to a digital-first, AI-mediated world. For today's children, saving may not occur in bank accounts but in stablecoins; borrowing may be driven by predictive cash flow models rather than blunt credit scores; and property may mean digital assets or fractional shares rather than brick-and-mortar ownership. If intergenerational advice fails to account for these systemic shifts, it risks becoming nostalgic rather than instructive.

The implications extend far beyond personal finance. Nations that embed systemic financial thinking into their curricula may produce citizens better equipped to navigate collective economic challenges—climate resilience, inequality, sovereign debt, and even AI regulation itself. Meanwhile, populations trained only in traditional numeracy may be outpaced not just by technology, but by those who *understand how technology shapes choices*. The divide here is not between rich and poor, but between *the system-aware and the system-oblivious.*

To prepare children for such a world is not merely to update syllabi. It is to rethink the very purpose of financial education. The old model aimed to create competent consumers and responsible savers. The new model aims to foster *adaptive thinkers*—people who can interrogate assumptions, collaborate with machines, and align automated systems with human values. This is not the abandonment of numeracy. It is its evolution into something broader, deeper, and more culturally vital.

Wealth education in the AI world must therefore become less about accumulating facts and more about cultivating insight. Less about memorising balance sheets and more about asking: *What does this system prioritise? Who benefits from this design? What's invisible in this data set?* These are not financial questions in the narrow sense. They are philosophical, systemic, and urgent. They are also the foundation for a new kind of literacy—one that speaks not only to dollars and data, but to agency, ethics, and design in an increasingly automated world.

"Stories Over Statements":

A last will and testament, no matter how precise, is fundamentally a blunt instrument. It distributes assets but rarely conveys values. It answers legal questions but not emotional ones. Why was a property left to one sibling and not another? What principles guided the decision to fund a scholarship rather than a trust? Traditional financial documents—statements, spreadsheets, and signed directives—are transactional by design. But legacy, as families increasingly recognise, is not just about transferring wealth. It is about transmitting *intention, context, and wisdom.* And artificial intelligence, long viewed as the executor of cold calculations, is now becoming an unlikely ally in making those inheritances more human.

We are witnessing a quiet but profound shift: from *documents* to *narratives*, from static instructions to dynamic storytelling. Families, estate planners, and technologists are beginning to use AI not merely to optimise wealth transfer, but to encode the emotional and ethical subtext behind financial decisions. The movement is still emerging, yet its implications are sweeping. As AI models become adept at contextualising data and generating natural language, they offer families a means to document not just what they did with their money—but *why* they did it, how they want it interpreted, and what they hope it might mean for future generations.

Consider a simple bequest—a sum left to a granddaughter with the stipulation that it be used "for education." In a traditional estate, this clause would trigger a compliance check: Is the tuition expense eligible? Does a certification programme count? But the clause says little about the spirit of the gift. Was it meant to fund university, or lifelong learning? Was it a nod to the family's tradition of self-education, or a response to the granddaughter's specific talents? Today, AI-powered platforms are enabling benefactors to attach stories, audio recordings, annotated timelines, and even AI-generated summaries of personal values to such gifts. These artefacts create a "narrative layer" over the financial directive—one that transforms inheritance from legal transaction into emotional dialogue.

This evolution is not sentimentalism. It's strategy. Research in behavioural economics shows that money is far more likely to be used in ways aligned with donor intention when recipients understand the motivation behind it. Families that contextualise their financial decisions—through letters, videos, or now, AI-assisted narratives—are statistically more likely to preserve intergenerational wealth and cohesion. The narrative creates not just clarity, but accountability. It offers descendants an interpretive framework, helping them make aligned decisions in future scenarios that the original documents could not anticipate.

AI is uniquely suited to scale this capability. Language models can transcribe and organise family histories, prompting users to fill in key moments, patterns, and inflection points. Sentiment analysis can detect tone, helping storytellers convey not just facts, but emotional cadence. AI agents can create dynamic legacy maps that link financial decisions to pivotal life events—such as the sale of a family business, the emigration of a grandparent, or the decision to fund a community initiative. Some platforms now allow users to simulate "what if" scenarios: What would Mum have thought about investing in cryptocurrency? Would Grandfather have approved of a green energy trust over a property portfolio? These speculative reconstructions are not infallible, but they offer an unprecedented approximation of voice and intent.

There are early institutional examples. In Singapore, a legal-tech startup is piloting "Legacy AI" services that record clients' financial philosophies alongside their estate plans. In Canada, intergenerational family offices are using natural language models to generate "family constitution drafts" that encapsulate shared values and adapt over time. In the United States, fintech startups like Helix Legacy and VaultPath allow families to store not only assets but *stories*—archived in secure, decentralised systems that heirs can access gradually through time-triggered or milestone-based releases. These technologies do not replace legal documentation, but they render it interpretable—emotionally legible in a way that PDFs and spreadsheets simply are not.

This raises critical questions about authorship, authenticity, and bias. Who owns the AI-generated story? If a patriarch revises his legacy narrative several times using different AI prompts, which version is "true"? How do we guard against revisionist storytelling—particularly in families where historical trauma or inequality is being smoothed over in curated narratives? And should heirs *trust* AI-mediated stories that might reflect the biases of both human input and machine learning architecture?

These concerns are real, but they are not unique to AI. Legacy narratives have always been contested. What AI introduces is *transparency of process*. Version histories, audit trails, and attribution protocols can be embedded into digital storytelling, allowing future readers to see not just the final text, but how it evolved—who wrote it, who revised it, what was added and omitted. Properly designed, this can become a tool for *intergenerational truth*, rather than distortion.

There are also deeper epistemic implications. For centuries, wealth was conveyed through fixed media—ledgers, title deeds, and eventually, digital records. These instruments excelled at precision but failed at interpretation. The emerging narrative layer, powered by AI, reverses that equation. It excels at nuance, context, and synthesis—but relies on intentional curation to avoid ambiguity. This tension is creative, not contradictory. A robust legacy is one that includes *both* the numbers and the narrative, the facts and the frame, the distribution and the deliberation.

For families, this represents an invitation to rethink what it means to pass something on. It is no longer sufficient to allocate capital; there is a rising expectation to explain capital. This includes articulating how wealth was built, what compromises were made, whom it was meant to empower, and how those aims might evolve. In a world where AI enables near-infinite replication of data but limited transmission of wisdom, the ability to craft *interpretable intention* may prove to be the most enduring form of wealth.

Financial advisors, estate planners, and AI technologists now face a new mandate: to design tools that are not only secure and compliant, but *narratively literate*. This will require collaboration across disciplines. Lawyers will need to work with storytellers. Programmers with philosophers. Families with facilitators. The goal is not merely a better document. It is a more meaningful inheritance.

At its core, the shift from statements to stories reflects a broader cultural re-evaluation of what matters in legacy. Money, alone, is an incomplete vessel. So are data, directives, and distribution algorithms. What gives inheritance its moral and psychological power is its narrative arc—the sense that one is not merely receiving *resources*, but stepping into a lineage, a purpose, a set of lived principles. AI, for all its flaws, offers us a new means to capture that arc. Not to automate legacy, but to animate it. Not to replace human voice, but to help it echo further, with context and clarity, into futures we cannot yet imagine.

Chapter 7
Collective Finance, Reimagined

A growing intuition—backed, increasingly, by data—suggests that wealth pursued in isolation has reached its limits. For much of the modern era, the scaffolding of finance rested on the solitary individual: retirement accounts tailored to a single name, portfolios optimised for one person's horizon, a private calculus of accumulation. Yet as interdependence deepens and volatility becomes the ambient condition of global life, this logic begins to falter. In its place, a more daring possibility comes into view: collective finance—systems consciously designed for shared futures, decentralised in structure, intelligent in operation, and tethered to common values.

This is not some wistful revival of communes or a naïve appeal to abolish private property. It is, rather, a pragmatic answer to the evident shortcomings of institutions that promised trust, transparency, and inclusion but failed to deliver them at scale. The pressing question is no longer abstract: what does it mean to manage money *together* in an age when machines can coordinate human intent with startling efficiency? The answers are emerging in blockchain cooperatives, AI-managed mutual pools, community housing funds run on smart contracts, and new species of digital public goods that blur the old boundary between citizen and investor.

Decentralised Autonomous Organisations—DAOs—mark a particularly vivid frontier. Once a niche experiment in crypto governance, they have evolved into laboratories of shared economic agency. Across art markets, farming co-ops, and activist circles, strangers converge to pool capital, deliberate proposals, and steer investments via code that is both transparent and binding. AI now threads through these systems, smoothing liquidity flows, running forecasts, even proposing policy options shaped by collective behaviour. What results is not a division of governance from investment but their fusion into a programmable, self-adjusting process.

Yet the true novelty here is not technological. It is philosophical. Traditional finance orbits around private gain; collective finance invites an alternative orientation—towards shared intentionality. It asks us to optimise not just for return, but for alignment: with a community, a mission, a generational aspiration. One might imagine freelance workers pooling part of their income into an AI-governed fund for parental leave. Or residents of a floodplain insuring themselves through a sensor-fed mutual scheme that adjusts in real time. These are not speculative sketches. They are happening, often quietly, beneath the radar of mainstream finance.

At the core of these experiments lies a reconfiguration of trust. Once, trust rested in institutions—banks, regulators, credentialed advisers. That scaffolding cracked long ago. The 2008 crisis was a rupture; subsequent years of data exploitation by fintechs and extractive incentives in public markets only deepened the fracture. Trust now migrates to protocol. Not decreed by authority, but earned through verifiability. In this reimagined landscape, AI does not reign as master but serves as referee—ensuring consistency, offering auditability, maintaining the feedback loops that allow collectives to adapt in motion.

Still, contradictions abound. Every algorithm embeds judgments: what counts as fair, what qualifies as sustainable, what risks are tolerable. A climate DAO must decide whether carbon credits are legitimate or a sleight of hand. A lending circle must weigh inclusivity against solvency. These are not just technical dilemmas; they are moral and cultural ones. Which is why AI in these contexts must aspire not only to execution but to interpretation—able to expose its assumptions, open them to contest, and allow human override where stakes demand it.

Here we encounter a new kind of commons. Historically, commons were forests, fisheries, grazing lands—resources governed through custom or law. Today, the commons is increasingly digital and financial: shared datasets, community-run platforms, pooled investment vehicles. Once the fear was overuse and depletion; now the challenge is subtler—ensuring collective assets adapt wisely, equitably, and with resilience. AI, in principle, can help: surfacing anomalies, simulating long-term effects, scaling participation. Whether it fulfils that promise depends on how it is embedded.

The pandemic offered glimpses of this dynamic. Informal mutual-aid networks sprang up across cities, routing groceries, medicine, and funds. Many now look to AI tools to manage fraud risks, anticipate surges in need, and guide resources more effectively. Likewise, local currencies—once quirky experiments—are finding renewed force through AI-backed contracts that guarantee liquidity, regulate exchange, and adapt to shifting community priorities. These are not just economic tools; they are civic infrastructures, stitched together by both human judgement and machine logic.

This movement also unsettles familiar narratives of economic success. The individualised measures—net worth, personal income, retirement sufficiency—no longer capture reality. Wealth lives within networks and ecosystems. Housing crises, supply chain fragility, climate shocks—none are navigable alone. Some collectives are already experimenting with alternative metrics: resilience scores, interdependence ratios, well-being indices. They may sound abstract, but they reflect the truth that value is not only personal but structural.

Even more provocatively, collective finance reshapes economic identity itself. In digital communities, often pseudonymous and transnational, participants are untethered from passports or banks. Instead, they cohere through protocols, pooled incentives, and shared goals. In such contexts, AI functions less as a cold calculator and more as a mediator—surfacing hidden tensions, modelling minority perspectives, and sometimes even suggesting new governance forms. Paradoxically, the injection of machine intelligence may open finance to greater plurality and responsiveness.

This inquiry, then, is not into redistribution but into redesign. From DAOs that underwrite cooperative investment to AI-augmented housing trusts; from ethical dilemmas coded into algorithms to the civic imagination of participatory finance—we are witnessing wealth being reconceived as something we build in common. The point is not to extinguish individual agency, but to embed it within frameworks that acknowledge interdependence and vulnerability alongside creativity and ambition.

None of this is without danger. Collective systems can concentrate power as swiftly as they can spread it. AI may obscure more than it reveals. Protocols meant for inclusion can ossify into echo chambers, or worse, digital hierarchies that replicate feudal patterns. These risks do not negate the project; they sharpen it. If intelligence is to make collaboration possible, collaboration must also make intelligence accountable.

We are, in truth, at a hinge in financial history. Distributed systems, machine learning, and civic imagination are converging into an architecture with transformative potential. The tools now exist not merely to optimise allocation but to choreograph cooperation. That is no minor shift. If the twentieth century was defined by the question of what an individual could earn alone, the twenty-first may hinge on what we are capable of building together. This exploration offers not a prediction but a provocation: a map of the questions we must learn to ask.

From Individual Portfolios to Shared Futures

Wealth, for most of modern financial history, has been a solitary enterprise. Retirement plans, stock picks, savings strategies—these have all been designed around the notion of individual optimisation. The underlying philosophy was clear: maximise personal gain, minimise personal risk, and treat others' financial decisions as background noise. That model still dominates retail finance platforms, robo-advisors, and mainstream investment advice. But it is beginning to fray. A confluence of technological, generational, and social shifts is reconfiguring how people think about money—not only as a private reserve, but as a shared tool for collective futures.

At the heart of this transformation is the emergence of *collaborative wealth design*: systems in which capital is not managed in isolation but pooled, programmed, and governed by groups with shared values, objectives, or identities. These are not mere investment clubs in digital drag. They represent a fundamental reimagining of the financial contract—from an individual transaction to a communal function. This reconfiguration is being made possible by three converging forces: decentralised digital infrastructure, participatory governance protocols, and artificial intelligence capable of managing complex, multi-stakeholder optimisation. Together, they are ushering in a model of finance that is as much about "we" as it is about "me."

Decentralised Autonomous Organisations (DAOs) exemplify this shift. At their core, DAOs are software-enabled collectives that manage resources through transparent rules encoded on a blockchain. Unlike traditional funds, they do not require intermediaries—no trustees, no fund managers, no central administrators. Instead, smart contracts handle decision execution, while participants vote on proposals using governance tokens. While early DAOs were primarily used for speculative crypto investments, the model has expanded dramatically. Today, there are DAOs focused on climate resilience, media cooperatives, digital art patronage, biotech research, and mutual aid. What binds them is not sector or strategy, but structure: *capital is co-owned, decisions are decentralised, and goals are democratically shaped.*

Yet DAOs are not the only form of collaborative capital. Crowd-investing platforms—fuelled by equity crowdfunding laws and new regulatory sandboxes—allow hundreds or thousands of individuals to co-invest in startups, real estate, and green energy. What once required institutional clout can now be achieved by a digitally networked crowd. These platforms are being enhanced by AI engines that analyse deal quality, assess participant sentiment, and optimise allocation algorithms to balance group preferences with project requirements. In effect, *AI becomes the invisible co-pilot*, ensuring that the wisdom of the crowd does not devolve into chaos or hype.

More radically, AI-managed *social wealth pools* are emerging as a distinct asset class. These pools resemble mutual funds in structure but differ in purpose. Instead of maximising return for a single investor, they optimise for collective outcomes: community resilience, affordable housing, regenerative agriculture, or access to education. AI models manage complex trade-offs—balancing capital growth with social impact metrics, dynamically adjusting allocations based on real-time feedback, and flagging risks before they cascade. These pools do not simply ask, "What's the best investment?" but rather, *"What's the most coherent expression of our shared values under current conditions?"*

Such developments demand a re-evaluation of familiar concepts. Risk, for instance, becomes relational. In a traditional portfolio, risk is abstracted and diversified—uncorrelated assets are good, volatility is to be smoothed. But in collaborative wealth systems, risk is also reputational, ethical, and systemic. A DAO that invests in fossil fuel infrastructure may outperform the market but lose the trust of its community. A crowd-funded real estate venture that gentrifies a neighbourhood may deliver returns but erode social capital. AI can help navigate these dilemmas, but only if its optimisation logic is *designed to accommodate plural outcomes* rather than binary success metrics.

Liquidity, too, becomes a more nuanced affair. In a shared future, capital is not always extractable on demand. Some DAOs impose lock-up periods to ensure stability. Others allow partial exits but only after passing governance review. These mechanisms force participants to grapple with an underexplored question in personal finance: *Is liquidity always good? Or are there forms of wealth that gain meaning through commitment?* In collaborative systems, money becomes less like water—flowing wherever returns are highest—and more like soil—anchored, tended, and stewarded for future growth.

This shift is not purely technological; it is generational. Millennials and Gen Z, raised amid financial crisis, student debt, and planetary crisis, often hold a more ambivalent view of wealth. Surveys indicate a preference for impact-aligned investing, co-ownership models, and participatory governance—even if it means lower or slower returns. They see finance not just as a means of personal security, but as an instrument for shaping collective destiny. Collaborative wealth platforms are emerging as the infrastructure to turn that preference into practice.

But they are not without tensions. The very openness that makes DAOs and social wealth pools attractive also makes them vulnerable: to coordination failures, governance capture, sybil attacks, and value drift. AI can mitigate some of these risks by flagging anomalies, simulating proposal outcomes, and modelling stakeholder sentiment. Yet AI itself is not neutral. Every algorithm contains embedded priorities—whether speed over fairness, growth over resilience, or majority over minority views. As these systems mature, *meta-governance*—the governance of the governance process—will become a core function. How do collectives decide what their AI should optimise for? Who trains the models? Who audits them? These are not side questions; they are the foundation of legitimacy.

Another challenge is cultural. Collaborative finance demands a new kind of financial literacy—one that is less about individual budgeting and more about systems thinking. Participants must understand not just assets and liabilities, but feedback loops, power dynamics, and emergent behaviour. This shift mirrors broader trends in education, where systems literacy is becoming as crucial as numerical or verbal proficiency. Collaborative wealth, then, is not just a financial model—it is a civic pedagogy.

Regulation, too, must evolve. Most legal frameworks assume that financial actors are discrete individuals or registered entities. DAOs challenge this premise. They exist across borders, often without legal personality or physical address. Similarly, crowd-investing platforms blur the lines between public offering and private placement. If regulation cannot keep pace, two outcomes are likely: either stifling compliance burdens that kill innovation, or grey zones where bad actors exploit legal ambiguity. Forward-looking jurisdictions are beginning to respond, offering *DAO charters, sandbox licenses, and digital cooperative statutes*—early signs of a legal architecture for the shared future.

Philosophically, collaborative wealth design reopens one of the oldest debates in economic thought: *What is capital for?* The individualist model says: to enable autonomy. The collectivist model says: to enable solidarity. The emerging view suggests a synthesis: *capital as a medium for co-creating meaningful futures*. In this view, investing is not a spectator sport or a zero-sum game—it is a form of participation in a story larger than oneself.

As AI, blockchain, and participatory finance converge, the architecture of wealth is being re-written. The ledger is no longer just a record of private gain. It is becoming a script of shared intention. And while the systems are still nascent—prone to failure, capture, and hype—the direction of travel is clear. Finance is no longer just personal. It is becoming *programmable, participatory, and plural.*

The challenge for practitioners, policymakers, and participants alike is to ensure that these tools do not simply replicate the inequities of legacy finance in new code. Instead, they must be designed to expand access, honour difference, and cultivate long-term thinking. That is the promise—and the provocation—of moving from individual portfolios to shared futures. Not just to make money differently, but to ask different questions about what wealth is, who it serves, and how it should be stewarded.

The New Commons –

The concept of the commons has long been associated with shared natural resources—forests, fisheries, grazing lands—that require collective stewardship to prevent depletion or degradation. Today, however, the commons is evolving beyond physical space and natural capital, extending into digital realms, social infrastructures, and financial ecosystems. At the forefront of this transformation is artificial intelligence, which communities worldwide are harnessing to manage resources democratically, balancing efficiency with equity and transparency. This reimagined commons is not merely about pooling assets; it represents a profound recalibration of how trust, governance, and participation intersect in the stewardship of shared wealth and wellbeing.

Housing stands as one of the most pressing arenas where AI-enabled commons are taking shape. Traditional property markets have become synonymous with exclusion, speculation, and volatility. In response, community land trusts, cooperative housing projects, and mutual aid collectives are turning to AI-driven platforms to administer resources more fairly and responsively. For example, algorithms can manage waitlists for affordable housing, optimising for factors such as urgency, community diversity, and stability. AI can also forecast neighbourhood dynamics, helping communities anticipate gentrification pressures or maintenance needs well before they escalate. Importantly, these systems are designed with participatory governance frameworks, ensuring that residents—not distant developers or landlords—retain decision-making power. This approach challenges the assumption that property management must be hierarchical and opaque, illustrating instead how technology can foster a more inclusive and proactive stewardship model.

Mutual aid networks, historically reliant on informal social ties and grassroots organisation, are also benefiting from AI's capacity to enhance coordination and transparency. During crises such as natural disasters or pandemics, timely allocation of resources can mean the difference between survival and hardship. AI platforms enable these networks to map needs, match volunteers, and track resource flows with unprecedented precision and speed. Moreover, by analysing patterns of community engagement and vulnerability, AI can suggest where to build resilience proactively rather than reactively. Yet these tools raise critical questions about privacy, autonomy, and surveillance: how much data should be shared in the name of collective wellbeing? Which decisions should remain human-led? These tensions underscore the importance of embedding ethical reflection into the design of AI for social commons, ensuring technology amplifies solidarity without compromising dignity or agency.

Local currencies and complementary monetary systems offer another compelling example of the AI-powered commons in action. Once niche experiments, local currencies are increasingly recognised as instruments for fostering economic resilience, recirculating wealth within communities, and supporting social enterprises. AI facilitates their scalability and adaptability by automating ledger management, detecting fraudulent activity, and dynamically adjusting currency supply to match economic conditions. For instance, some cities have piloted AI-backed time banks, where residents exchange services recorded and managed by transparent algorithms. This decentralised approach counters the monopolistic tendencies of national currencies, inviting a plurality of economic practices attuned to local values and needs. Yet the success of these systems hinges on trust—trust that the algorithms governing them are fair, comprehensible, and accountable. As such, transparency protocols and participatory oversight are critical components, highlighting that the commons cannot be managed by AI alone but require a partnership between human judgement and machine intelligence.

Despite these advances, the deployment of AI within communal resource management is not without challenges. One significant concern is the risk of reproducing or amplifying existing inequalities. AI systems trained on historical data can inadvertently embed biases, privileging certain groups while marginalising others. In housing allocation, for instance, poorly designed algorithms might reinforce segregation or exclude vulnerable populations. Likewise, mutual aid networks dependent on digital platforms risk excluding those with limited internet access or technological literacy. Addressing these issues demands intentional design choices, such as incorporating fairness constraints, ensuring algorithmic explainability, and facilitating inclusive participation in governance. Moreover, the commons ethos itself must expand to encompass digital justice as an integral pillar.

Another critical tension lies in balancing efficiency with democratic deliberation. AI excels at processing vast data and optimising for predefined objectives, yet communal resource management often involves competing values, plural interests, and fluid priorities that resist algorithmic reduction. For the commons to flourish, AI tools must be conceived not as arbiters but as facilitators—augmenting human decision-making without supplanting it. This means fostering interfaces that enable participants to understand, contest, and co-create the criteria driving resource allocation. It also entails cultivating digital literacy and collective capacity, so communities are equipped to steward both technology and trust.

The new commons, enabled by AI, also challenge conventional notions of property and ownership. Rather than exclusive possession, value is increasingly derived from participation, stewardship, and shared benefit. Blockchain-based platforms, for example, are experimenting with tokenised governance rights that distribute control proportionally among community members. This model disrupts entrenched hierarchies, enabling more fluid and accountable management of resources. Yet it also demands new legal and institutional frameworks to recognise and protect these forms of collective ownership. The ongoing dialogue between technologists, policymakers, and community organisers is critical to shaping an ecosystem where AI-enhanced commons can thrive sustainably.

In essence, AI's role in managing the commons is neither a panacea nor a threat—it is an enabler whose promise depends on how it is wielded. When designed with transparency, inclusivity, and ethical foresight, AI can help communities transcend the limitations of scale and complexity that have historically constrained collective action. By automating routine tasks, providing predictive insights, and facilitating coordination, AI frees human agency to focus on the relational, moral, and creative dimensions of stewardship. Conversely, neglecting these human factors risks technocratic overreach and alienation.

As we stand at the cusp of this transformation, it is imperative to recognise that the commons is as much about social imagination as it is about technology. The aspiration is to craft systems where resources are not merely owned or consumed but co-managed as expressions of shared responsibility and mutual flourishing. The new commons promise a richer, more resilient financial ecology—one where wealth circulates in service of communities, where AI amplifies democratic governance rather than centralises control, and where the architecture of resource management reflects the complexity and diversity of human life. This chapter charts the contours of this evolving landscape, exploring both its dazzling potentials and profound challenges, inviting readers to rethink what it means to steward wealth together in a networked, algorithmic world.

AI as a Governance Tool –

Artificial intelligence is often framed as a tool for automating tasks, optimising portfolios, or detecting fraud in financial services. Yet one of its most profound, if less heralded, applications lies in its capacity to transform governance—particularly collective decision-making within finance. As financial ecosystems grow ever more complex and interconnected, the traditional mechanisms for managing shared resources and communal risk struggle to keep pace.

Machine learning and related AI techniques are now emerging as indispensable instruments in crafting governance models that are more transparent, accountable, and responsive. This subchapter explores how AI functions not merely as an analytical engine, but as a catalyst for reinventing the social architecture of finance itself.

The governance challenges facing contemporary finance are formidable. Consider decentralised autonomous organisations (DAOs), which pool capital and delegate decisions to distributed participants. Unlike conventional firms with hierarchical boards, DAOs rely on consensus protocols, token-weighted voting, and open-source rulebooks. While ideologically democratic, this model quickly runs into practical limitations: voter apathy, coordination failures, and the tyranny of the majority. AI offers solutions by augmenting collective intelligence, distilling vast streams of input into coherent patterns, and simulating outcomes of competing proposals. Machine learning algorithms can detect latent conflicts, identify influential actors, and flag governance processes vulnerable to manipulation or capture. In this way, AI serves as a *guardian of procedural integrity*—not replacing human judgment, but enhancing it through computational rigor.

Transparency is a cornerstone of legitimate governance, yet paradoxically, as systems become more complex, understanding diminishes. Financial contracts embedded in code, multi-layered incentive structures, and interdependent risk exposures defy casual scrutiny. AI-powered visualisation and natural language generation tools help bridge this gap by translating raw data and intricate logic into accessible narratives and dashboards. For example, platforms like Snapshot—a popular DAO voting interface—integrate AI-driven analytics to present proposal impacts, stakeholder sentiment, and historical voting behaviours. This empowers participants to make informed decisions, fostering an environment where transparency is not a passive disclosure but an active engagement. Here, AI democratizes expertise, flattening knowledge asymmetries that traditionally favoured institutional actors.

Accountability, closely tied to transparency, benefits similarly from AI-enabled traceability. Distributed ledger technologies record every transaction, vote, and policy change immutably, yet the sheer volume of records can obscure patterns of influence or irregularity. Machine learning algorithms excel at anomaly detection, uncovering unusual voting blocs or coordinated behaviour suggestive of collusion. Beyond policing, AI can proactively recommend corrective actions or propose alternative governance structures that balance power more equitably. In traditional financial institutions, compliance departments have begun deploying AI for risk monitoring and audit trails, but within collaborative finance, these tools are part of the very fabric of governance, embedded from inception to ensure continual vigilance.

However, this integration of AI into governance raises profound questions about agency and trust. When decision-making is assisted—or in some cases partially delegated—to algorithms, who is responsible for outcomes? How transparent must the AI's logic be to warrant confidence from participants? These concerns fuel the development of *explainable AI* (XAI) within governance frameworks, where models are designed to produce human-interpretable rationales for their suggestions or flags. This approach counters the "black box" problem, enhancing legitimacy by enabling communities to interrogate, challenge, or refine algorithmic input. Moreover, participatory design practices involve stakeholders in co-creating AI governance tools, ensuring the technology reflects collective values rather than inscrutable mandates.

The intersection of AI and governance also opens opportunities to explore novel decision-making paradigms. Traditional voting systems privilege quantity over quality, often marginalising minority perspectives. AI can support *deliberative democracy* models, where machine learning curates diverse viewpoints, models consensus-building processes, and proposes compromises. Through sentiment analysis, topic modelling, and predictive simulations, AI facilitates a richer discourse that transcends binary choices. This capacity is particularly valuable in financial contexts where decisions carry multifaceted social and ethical implications beyond mere profit maximisation.

Real-world applications illustrate the transformative potential and attendant complexities. The Aragon Network, a pioneering DAO platform, employs AI tools to moderate governance forums, summarise debates, and detect governance attacks. Similarly, the DAOstack framework integrates machine learning to optimise proposal prioritisation, balancing stakeholder interests and resource constraints. On the regulatory front, jurisdictions such as Switzerland and Singapore are experimenting with AI-supported supervisory technologies ("suptech") that monitor blockchain-based financial entities in real time, enhancing oversight without stifling innovation. These examples underscore a future where AI and humans co-govern increasingly hybridised financial commons.

Nonetheless, challenges remain. Data quality is paramount; governance AI depends on comprehensive, accurate, and unbiased datasets. Incomplete or skewed information can perpetuate systemic inequalities or misdirect decision-making. Additionally, governance systems are inherently political arenas where values conflict; AI's optimisation algorithms may inadvertently privilege dominant perspectives unless explicitly designed for pluralism and fairness. Furthermore, the risk of technocratic overreach looms if communities defer too readily to algorithmic authority, undermining democratic participation. The solution lies not in AI supremacy, but in *augmented governance*—a partnership where AI amplifies human capacities while remaining subject to human accountability.

Ethical reflection must also consider the implications of automating aspects of trust and authority. Historically, finance has relied on intermediaries—bankers, advisors, regulators—who embodied institutional trust. AI challenges this model by decentralising and codifying trust relationships through transparent, algorithmic means. This transition requires a reimagining of trust as a socio-technical construct, co-produced by humans and machines. Building trust in AI governance demands rigorous standards for fairness, explainability, and user consent, alongside ongoing community engagement and education.

As finance continues its evolution from centralised institutions to decentralised networks, AI as a governance tool stands at the crossroads of innovation and responsibility. It offers unparalleled possibilities to democratise access, enhance accountability, and sustain complex collective endeavours. Yet realising this potential requires vigilance against new forms of exclusion and control, thoughtful integration of human values, and a commitment to transparency that transcends technical sophistication. The governance architectures emerging today will shape not only financial outcomes but the social contracts of tomorrow's interconnected world. Understanding and engaging with AI's role in this domain is thus not optional—it is essential for anyone invested in the future of finance.

Trust, Community, and the Post-Institutional Era –

Trust in finance has long been anchored in centralised institutions—banks, regulatory agencies, insurance companies, and fund managers—entities that claim authority through legal mandates, capital reserves, and reputational capital. These institutions functioned as the gatekeepers of wealth creation, risk management, and capital allocation, offering assurance to individuals and organisations alike. Yet the fabric of this trust is unraveling, challenged not only by technological disruption but by shifting social dynamics. The rise of decentralised, tech-augmented communities—tribes bound not by geography or legacy institutions but by shared purpose and digital protocols—is reshaping the foundation of financial trust. This transformation signals a post-institutional era, where trust is increasingly mediated through algorithms, collective governance, and peer-to-peer networks.

The traditional trust model rests on three pillars: legal enforceability, institutional stability, and transparent oversight. For decades, these pillars sustained confidence in financial systems, even as occasional failures prompted reforms. Yet systemic crises, regulatory gaps, and perceived conflicts of interest have eroded public faith in centralised entities. Moreover, the accelerating pace of technological innovation and the complexity of global finance have outstripped the ability of single institutions to govern effectively. Against this backdrop, decentralised models—enabled by blockchain technology, smart contracts, and AI-driven governance—offer a compelling alternative. They promise *trust through transparency and automation*, reducing reliance on opaque intermediaries while empowering communities to co-create financial frameworks aligned with their values.

Decentralised Autonomous Organisations (DAOs) epitomise this shift. By encoding governance rules into smart contracts, DAOs enable members to propose, vote on, and execute decisions collectively, with every action recorded immutably on a blockchain. This structure replaces hierarchical authority with algorithmic enforcement, fostering a trust architecture grounded in verifiable code rather than institutional fiat. The growing adoption of DAOs for venture capital, social impact projects, and community investment illustrates a migration from individual portfolios to shared economic futures governed by digital tribes. Here, trust is less about personal relationships or brand reputation and more about the integrity and resilience of the underlying protocol.

However, technology alone does not create trust. The "techno-optimism" that celebrated decentralisation often underestimated the social and cultural dimensions critical to trust formation. Human networks, communal norms, and shared narratives remain essential. Digital tribes harness AI and machine learning not only to execute transactions but to facilitate communication, mediate disputes, and cultivate mutual accountability. For instance, sentiment analysis tools gauge community mood around proposals, while reputation systems reward constructive participation. These mechanisms augment traditional social capital with data-driven insights, creating a hybrid model where trust is co-produced by humans and machines.

This evolution is particularly salient in the context of financial inclusion and global diaspora communities. Digital-native populations, remote workers, and borderless entrepreneurs increasingly rely on tech-augmented tribes for financial services outside conventional banking. Mobile money platforms like M-Pesa in Kenya, combined with blockchain-based remittances, demonstrate how trust is reconstructed through interoperable, community-governed systems rather than state-backed currencies or institutions. Similarly, crowdfunding platforms leveraging AI moderation and smart contracts empower niche interest groups to pool resources for ventures aligned with shared values. These examples illustrate *the decentralisation of financial trust as both a technological and social phenomenon*, dissolving barriers imposed by geography, regulation, and traditional creditworthiness assessments.

Yet the post-institutional trust landscape is neither uniform nor uncontested. Challenges abound in governance design, security, and inclusivity. DAOs, while transparent, face dilemmas of voter apathy and concentration of power among token whales. Algorithmic decision-making risks embedding biases or excluding non-technical participants. Moreover, regulatory ambiguity leaves questions about legal recourse and protection unresolved. Trust in decentralised finance (DeFi) thus hinges on developing robust frameworks for accountability, dispute resolution, and ethical oversight that integrate technological safeguards with participatory governance.

Philosophically, this shift prompts reflection on the nature of trust itself. Classical theories emphasise trust as a relational construct built over time through repeated interactions and mutual vulnerability. In contrast, the post-institutional model extends trust to *systems*—networks of protocols, code, and distributed consensus. This system-trust requires new literacies: understanding algorithmic transparency, recognising governance tokens' implications, and critically engaging with automated enforcement. Financial literacy must expand to encompass *digital fluency* in trust architectures, enabling individuals not only to participate but to shape these evolving ecosystems.

The implications for social cohesion are profound. As trust disperses from centralised authorities to decentralised tribes, financial communities may become more fragmented yet simultaneously more aligned with members' identities and aspirations. This raises both opportunities and risks. On one hand, personalised, value-driven financial collectives can foster innovation, resilience, and empowerment. On the other, the potential for echo chambers, exclusionary practices, and governance gridlock intensifies. The design of inclusive, adaptable trust frameworks will be critical to harnessing AI-augmented tribal finance for collective prosperity rather than division.

Practitioners and policymakers face a formidable mandate. Facilitating this transition requires nurturing environments where decentralised trust can flourish without sacrificing stability or equity. This involves collaborative innovation in legal standards, interoperability protocols, and ethical AI deployment. Initiatives such as the Blockchain Trust Accelerator and international regulatory sandboxes exemplify efforts to balance experimentation with consumer protection. Furthermore, interdisciplinary dialogue drawing from sociology, computer science, and finance is essential to decode the multifaceted dynamics of trust in a networked age.

In sum, the post-institutional era represents a paradigmatic shift in the social infrastructure of finance. Trust is migrating from singular, centralised bastions to plural, decentralised, tech-augmented tribes that redefine how individuals relate to money, risk, and collective agency. This transformation challenges long-held assumptions about authority, transparency, and community, demanding new modes of engagement and governance. Embracing this shift offers the possibility of more resilient, participatory, and values-aligned financial systems—provided we attend as carefully to the human dimensions of trust as to the algorithms that now mediate it.

Chapter 8
The New Alchemy – Redefining Value

Value has never been fixed. It bends and shifts with the currents of culture, economy, and technology. Yet rarely, if ever, has its meaning undergone a recalibration as radical as the one now unfolding. Artificial intelligence does not simply process wealth; it reconfigures our very sense of what counts as wealth. The medieval alchemists dreamed of turning lead into gold; today's transmutation is subtler but more audacious, happening in the digital sphere. Here, data crystallises into assets, behaviours become tradable signals, and qualities once considered ineffable—creativity, identity, even emotion—are rendered as measurable currencies. What follows is an inquiry into this metamorphosis: how AI expands the dimensions of value while forcing us to reckon with the moral frameworks that underwrite valuation itself.

The most striking development is the elevation of personal data into a primary asset class. Once, wealth was tethered to tangible holdings—land, minerals, capital goods. Now, the seams of value run through human experience. Every click, glance, or hesitation provides fuel for algorithmic models that treat ephemeral gestures as market signals. Companies such as Palantir or Nielsen helped pioneer this commodification, while Facebook and Google have perfected the extraction of identity for the surgical precision of advertising. More unsettling still, AI has moved beyond demographics into the parsing of emotion itself: facial expressions, vocal inflections, heart-rate variability. A raised eyebrow, a tremor in tone—these become predictive inputs with monetary weight. In such a landscape, the human self is no longer merely expressive; it is capitalisable.

This raises questions we can scarcely afford to ignore. Who owns this data? How meaningful is consent when the very cues being harvested are involuntary or subconscious? And what becomes of human complexity when it is flattened into transactional fragments? The conversion of experience into asset is not just a technical act—it is political and ethical. Without frameworks of transparency, ownership, and equitable redistribution, this new economy risks becoming an engine of extraction rather than empowerment.

Running alongside the data revolution is another transformation: the redefinition of success itself. Gross Domestic Product—our canonical measure of prosperity—counts production but omits wellbeing. AI, with its appetite for multidimensional data, offers the possibility of weaving new measures into our collective calculus: health, longevity, purpose, community. Initiatives like the OECD's Better Life Index and AI-driven longevity research are early signs of this shift. Algorithms trained on social connectivity, environmental quality, and mental resilience sit alongside income charts, sketching wealth as a portfolio of life quality rather than a stack of numbers.

But translating this vision into practice is fraught. How does one weigh subjective experience against cold data points? How do we respect cultural variation in definitions of "wellbeing" while still producing metrics that guide action? And how do we prevent technocratic optimisation from disguising itself as benevolence? Here AI is a paradox: it offers unprecedented scope for nuance, yet also heightens the risk of reductionism.

Meanwhile, intangible forms of wealth—creativity, social networks, cultural presence—are stepping to the centre of economic life. The creator economy, the monetisation of influence, the speculative fervour around NFTs all signal a marketplace where human expression itself is financialised. AI enables this by mapping the subtleties of influence and creativity, modelling patterns once invisible. Traditional finance, long preoccupied with balance sheets and cash flow, is being pressed to account for these softer yet potent forms of capital.

And yet, there is danger in this commodification of the intangible. When identity becomes collateral, how do we protect authenticity from erosion? How do we draw lines between empowerment and exploitation? A poem, a photograph, a reputation—all can be sold. But can they be preserved as meaningful once converted into assets? The tension between monetisation and meaning lies at the heart of this new economy, demanding careful negotiation rather than blind embrace.

Beneath all of this lies the act of valuation itself. To assign worth is never neutral—it is always a moral, often philosophical exercise. From Aristotle's insistence on virtue to Rawls's notion of fairness, valuation reflects the priorities of the time. AI does not erase this truth; it intensifies it. Algorithms are not empty vessels. They carry the values, blind spots, and ambitions of their makers. As we entrust them with shaping markets and futures, embedding ethical reflection into their design is not optional—it is essential. Fairness constraints, transparency tools, diverse governance models: these are not afterthoughts but preconditions for legitimacy.

The consequences are sweeping. If valuation is moral at its core, it requires vigilance and humility. It demands that societies interrogate what they wish to prioritise, what legacies they hope to leave, and how they will guard against the narrowing of human richness into numbers alone. AI, as a kind of modern alchemist, offers immense power to refashion economies and lives. But whether the gold it yields is just, or merely plentiful, depends on the frameworks we weave around it.

What lies ahead is not merely a technical shift but a cultural reorientation. Value now stretches beyond accumulation into realms of data, wellbeing, creativity, and ethics. To navigate this new terrain requires curiosity tempered by scepticism, imagination tethered to responsibility. The question is no longer only what is valuable, but *why*—and by whose measure. In that inquiry, the role of AI will be decisive, but never final. The ultimate answers must remain human.

When Data Becomes Asset –

The transformation of personal data into a financial asset represents one of the most profound shifts in the modern economy. While data has long underpinned business decisions and targeted marketing, the advent of sophisticated artificial intelligence has elevated this resource to unprecedented prominence. AI now parses not only explicit consumer behaviour but also the subtle nuances of identity, emotion, and social interaction, converting them into quantifiable inputs with direct monetary value. This metamorphosis—from intangible information to tangible asset—raises critical questions about ownership, privacy, and the very nature of human worth in a digitised world. Understanding this evolution is essential for anyone engaged with finance, technology, or the broader societal impact of data commodification.

The process begins with recognising that data is not a monolith but a complex mosaic of personal attributes. Traditional analytics relied heavily on demographic or transactional data—age, income, purchase history—to predict behaviour. Contemporary AI systems integrate these with behavioural signals, psychological profiles, and biometric data, constructing multi-dimensional representations of individuals. For example, fintech platforms employ machine learning models to assess creditworthiness not solely from credit scores but also by analysing patterns of social media activity, spending habits, and even emotional indicators derived from facial recognition technology. This multidimensional profiling transforms abstract personal traits into actionable insights, allowing financial institutions to tailor products, pricing, and risk assessment with unprecedented precision.

Monetisation arises from this precision. Companies that can decode behavioural and emotional data unlock new revenue streams through hyper-targeted advertising, personalised financial advice, and dynamic pricing models. A salient example is the burgeoning field of behavioural finance apps that nudge users towards investment or saving behaviours aligned with their psychological predispositions. By embedding AI that interprets real-time emotional states or social influences, these platforms optimise user engagement and profitability. The capacity to quantify the "soft" aspects of human experience—such as stress levels or aspirational identity—turns once intangible elements into commodities, traded within digital ecosystems as currency for influence and capital allocation.

Yet, this transformation is far from unproblematic. The reduction of identity and emotion to data points risks dehumanising complex inner lives, transforming individuals into mere algorithmic variables. This commodification presents significant ethical challenges. Who controls this data, and who profits from it? The phenomenon of "data exhaust"—the inadvertent trail of personal information generated by everyday activities—raises concerns over consent and autonomy. Often, individuals are unaware of the extent to which their behaviour is monitored and monetised. High-profile controversies such as the Cambridge Analytica scandal exemplify the potential for misuse, demonstrating how data-driven insights can be weaponised to manipulate political opinions or consumer choices. These incidents underscore the urgency of developing robust frameworks for data governance that balance innovation with individual rights.

Moreover, the economic consequences of data monetisation are complex. While data-driven insights can democratise access to financial products by refining risk models and lowering barriers, they may also exacerbate inequalities. Algorithms trained on biased datasets risk perpetuating discriminatory practices, particularly in credit scoring or insurance underwriting. Marginalised groups may find themselves unfairly excluded or overcharged based on proxies derived from behavioural data, reinforcing systemic disparities. The opacity of many AI models compounds this problem, making it difficult for consumers or regulators to challenge unjust outcomes. Addressing these challenges requires transparency initiatives, explainability in AI, and participatory design processes that incorporate diverse stakeholder perspectives.

The monetisation of emotion marks a particularly sensitive frontier. Advances in affective computing enable AI to detect and respond to emotional cues with remarkable accuracy, informing decisions ranging from personalised marketing to mental health interventions. While these capabilities offer potential benefits—such as tailored financial advice during periods of stress—they also invite ethical dilemmas concerning emotional privacy and manipulation. For instance, if a robo-advisor adjusts investment recommendations based on detected anxiety, does this empower the client or exploit vulnerability? The line between support and surveillance blurs, demanding rigorous ethical scrutiny and safeguards to protect users' emotional integrity.

In practical terms, the financialisation of personal data requires new literacy among consumers and professionals alike. Users must understand how their data is collected, analysed, and monetised, and what trade-offs this entails for privacy and agency. Financial advisors and planners face the challenge of interpreting AI-generated insights that incorporate behavioural and emotional dimensions, integrating these with human judgement to serve clients' broader goals. Regulators, for their part, must develop policies that foster innovation while preventing abuse, such as mandating data portability, consent protocols, and algorithmic audits.

Real-world applications provide instructive case studies. Companies like Experian and FICO have expanded traditional credit scoring by incorporating alternative data, including mobile phone usage and social behaviour, enabling credit access for underserved populations. Meanwhile, emerging platforms like the Brave browser reward users with cryptocurrency for attention and data sharing, flipping the traditional data-for-profit model by compensating individuals directly. These innovations hint at new paradigms where data ownership and value capture may shift towards individuals, challenging existing corporate monopolies over personal information.

Nonetheless, the trajectory of data as asset is neither linear nor predetermined. Cultural, legal, and technological contexts shape how this alchemy unfolds. The European Union's General Data Protection Regulation (GDPR) exemplifies a regulatory approach that foregrounds individual rights and data sovereignty, influencing global standards and corporate behaviour. Contrastingly, more laissez-faire regimes may accelerate commodification but risk deepening asymmetries. Societal debates about the ethical limits of data use, including calls for "data dignity," reveal growing awareness of the profound stakes involved.

As AI continues to weave behaviour, identity, and emotion into financial models, it challenges foundational assumptions about what constitutes wealth and value. The commodification of personal data reframes human attributes as marketable assets, transforming everyday life into a domain of economic calculation. This development offers both unprecedented opportunities for personalised services and troubling risks of surveillance, inequality, and dehumanisation. Navigating this terrain demands not only technical expertise but also ethical vigilance, multidisciplinary collaboration, and inclusive dialogue.

For readers invested in the future of finance and society, grappling with the implications of data monetisation is indispensable. It requires moving beyond simplistic narratives of innovation or dystopia towards nuanced understanding of how AI reshapes the economy's very fabric. By examining the mechanics, applications, and ethical dimensions of turning data into asset, this chapter equips readers with the conceptual tools to engage critically and constructively with the emergent data economy—one that holds transformative potential for individuals, institutions, and communities alike.

Beyond GDP: AI and Wellbeing Metrics –

The conventional measures of economic success have long been anchored to the gross domestic product (GDP), a quantitative index representing the total value of goods and services produced within a country. While GDP provides an indispensable gauge of economic activity, its limitations have become increasingly apparent. It neglects crucial dimensions of human experience such as wellbeing, longevity, mental health, and purpose—factors that profoundly shape quality of life yet evade simplistic numerical capture. Artificial intelligence now offers a transformative avenue to bridge this gap. By harnessing vast, multifaceted data streams and sophisticated analytical tools, AI is enabling the measurement and integration of non-financial success metrics into financial planning and policy frameworks. This development challenges traditional paradigms, inviting a more holistic and human-centred understanding of wealth and prosperity.

At the core of this shift is a recognition that wellbeing transcends material accumulation. Historical attempts to measure wellbeing—such as the Human Development Index or Bhutan's Gross National Happiness—have laid groundwork but often rely on limited datasets and periodic surveys. AI, by contrast, thrives on dynamic, real-time information drawn from diverse sources: wearable health devices, social media sentiment, environmental sensors, and more. For instance, machine learning algorithms can analyse heart rate variability, sleep patterns, and activity levels to produce granular assessments of physical health and stress. Simultaneously, natural language processing interprets textual and vocal cues indicative of mental states. By synthesising these data, AI constructs nuanced profiles of individual and population wellbeing, capable of informing personalised financial strategies attuned not just to wealth accumulation but to sustaining health and happiness over time.

A particularly compelling application lies in longevity forecasting. Advances in biogerontology and predictive analytics allow AI systems to estimate life expectancy more accurately by integrating genetic, behavioural, and environmental factors. This enables financial planners to tailor retirement savings, healthcare provisioning, and insurance coverage with unprecedented precision. The implications extend beyond individual portfolios; policymakers can deploy AI-generated longevity models to design social safety nets and allocate resources more efficiently. This convergence of health data and finance underscores a paradigm where economic planning must be intimately tied to biological realities and aspirations for a fulfilling lifespan.

Mental health, long marginalised in economic discourse, is now entering the financial lexicon through AI-enabled metrics. Depression, anxiety, and cognitive decline exert substantial economic costs yet resist conventional quantification. AI platforms analysing digital footprints—patterns of communication, online behaviour, and biometric indicators—offer early detection and continuous monitoring of mental wellbeing. These insights inform interventions that preserve cognitive function and emotional resilience, essential components of sustained productivity and financial security. Financial institutions increasingly recognise that supporting clients' mental health aligns with prudent risk management and client retention, signalling a shift from transactional relationships to holistic stewardship.

Purpose and meaning present an even more elusive frontier for quantification. Yet AI-driven sentiment analysis and social network examination can infer individual and community engagement levels, values alignment, and social capital. Incorporating such qualitative data into financial planning enriches the understanding of what constitutes success for clients beyond balance sheets. This approach fosters alignment between financial goals and personal fulfilment, promoting investments in education, philanthropy, or entrepreneurial ventures that resonate with clients' identities and aspirations.

The integration of wellbeing metrics into planning models raises profound conceptual and ethical considerations. First, the multiplicity of wellbeing dimensions demands sophisticated weighting and trade-off decisions. How should mental health be prioritised relative to longevity or financial security? AI models must be transparent and adaptable, reflecting clients' values rather than imposing monolithic criteria. This underscores the need for human oversight and participatory design in algorithm development to prevent technocratic determinism.

Second, the collection and utilisation of intimate personal data necessitate rigorous privacy protections and informed consent. The sensitive nature of health and emotional information heightens risks of misuse or discrimination. Robust governance frameworks are essential to safeguard individual rights while enabling beneficial innovation.

Third, cultural and contextual variability in wellbeing perceptions challenges universal metric design. AI systems must accommodate diverse conceptions of flourishing, avoiding ethnocentric biases. Cross-disciplinary collaboration involving social scientists, ethicists, and local communities enhances the cultural competence of wellbeing models.

Real-world initiatives exemplify the potential of AI-augmented wellbeing metrics. The OECD's Better Life Index incorporates subjective wellbeing indicators to complement economic statistics, informing national policy. Start-ups such as Life.io integrate behavioural science and AI to incentivise healthy lifestyles with financial rewards. Health insurers increasingly deploy AI to personalise premiums based on holistic health assessments. These applications demonstrate a convergence of technology, finance, and human-centric values reshaping economic planning.

Nevertheless, skepticism persists regarding the feasibility and desirability of quantifying such complex phenomena. Critics caution against reductionism—the risk that rich human experiences are flattened into algorithmic outputs that obscure nuance. Others warn of surveillance capitalism and the commodification of wellbeing data. These critiques highlight the imperative for ethical frameworks ensuring that AI serves to empower rather than exploit individuals.

For professionals and learners engaged with the evolving landscape of finance, understanding the integration of AI-driven wellbeing metrics is imperative. This knowledge enables more informed, compassionate, and effective engagement with clients and policies that recognise the multifaceted nature of human prosperity. It encourages a reimagining of financial success not as an end in itself but as a means to fostering meaningful, healthy, and purposeful lives.

Ultimately, the shift beyond GDP catalysed by AI reflects a broader societal evolution—towards economies and institutions that honour complexity, embrace interdisciplinarity, and centre the human experience. Engaging critically and constructively with these developments offers the promise of financial systems attuned to the true dimensions of wellbeing, capable of supporting flourishing individuals and communities in an increasingly complex world.

Art, Expression, and the Rise of Intangible Wealth –

The rise of intangible wealth marks one of the most profound shifts in how value is conceived and managed in the contemporary financial landscape. Historically, wealth was primarily associated with tangible assets: land, buildings, commodities, and physical currency. However, the rapid advancement of artificial intelligence has accelerated a transformation wherein *creative output*, *personal identity*, and *network capital* emerge as significant—and increasingly quantifiable—forms of capital. This evolution compels a reevaluation of traditional financial planning, challenging professionals and investors to recognise and incorporate these less visible but deeply influential dimensions of value.

Creative output, long relegated to the realm of art and culture as expressions of individual or collective imagination, now occupies a strategic place in economic portfolios. The digital age has enabled creators—from musicians and visual artists to writers and designers—to monetise their work beyond conventional sales and royalties. AI-powered platforms analyse audience engagement, predict trends, and optimise distribution, effectively transforming creativity into a measurable asset. For example, algorithms embedded in music streaming services assess listener patterns to forecast the commercial potential of new tracks, influencing investment in artists and projects. Similarly, AI-driven tools assist visual artists by identifying market demand and even generating derivative artworks that can enhance an original creator's brand and income streams. This confluence of art and algorithmic insight creates a new dynamic where creativity is not only an expression of identity but also a strategic asset in wealth management.

The concept of identity itself has expanded into a form of capital in the AI era. Personal branding, reputation, and digital presence are quantifiable assets that carry real economic weight. Social media influencers exemplify this phenomenon: their follower counts, engagement rates, and content resonance translate directly into monetisable opportunities such as sponsorships, merchandise, and exclusive access offerings. AI systems track and predict the trajectory of these personal brands, enabling investors and managers to assess and leverage identity capital. Furthermore, identity intertwines with authenticity and trust—qualities that AI algorithms evaluate through sentiment analysis and behavioural data. The capacity to craft and sustain a digital identity, supported by AI-driven analytics, is becoming central to individual financial strategies, particularly for entrepreneurs and freelancers whose brand equity fuels their economic prospects.

Network capital—the value derived from social connections, collaborations, and community influence—is another intangible asset gaining prominence. Advances in AI allow for sophisticated mapping and quantification of networks, revealing the structural and functional roles individuals play within professional, social, and economic ecosystems. This information informs decisions about partnerships, investments, and resource allocation. For instance, venture capital firms increasingly utilise AI to assess not only a startup's financial metrics but also the founders' network strength and influence within relevant industries. Platforms that facilitate crowd-investing or social lending use AI to match borrowers with lenders by analysing shared interests, mutual contacts, and historical reliability, thereby reducing risk and expanding access to capital. In this way, network capital transcends mere social currency, becoming a vital component of financial planning and risk assessment.

The integration of intangible wealth into AI-era financial planning introduces conceptual tensions and practical challenges. Unlike traditional assets, intangible wealth resists straightforward valuation, fluctuates with cultural and technological trends, and is often deeply subjective. This complexity demands that financial professionals develop new expertise to interpret AI-generated insights critically and ethically. They must navigate between overreliance on algorithmic outputs—which risk oversimplification or bias—and the nuanced understanding of human creativity, identity, and relationships.

Moreover, ethical considerations arise around data privacy, consent, and the commodification of personal and creative expression. The quantification of identity and network capital entails the collection and analysis of extensive personal data, raising concerns about surveillance, autonomy, and equity. Transparency in how AI systems evaluate intangible assets is essential to maintain trust and protect individuals from exploitation. At the same time, the democratization of tools for creative production and network building through AI can empower diverse populations, expanding participation in wealth creation beyond traditional gatekeepers.

Real-world applications illustrate the transformative potential of intangible wealth. The burgeoning market for non-fungible tokens (NFTs) exemplifies how creative digital assets can command significant financial value, with AI facilitating authentication, provenance tracking, and market analysis. In the realm of social entrepreneurship, AI supports the mobilisation of community networks and identity-driven campaigns that generate both social impact and economic returns. Financial advisory firms are incorporating AI-driven sentiment and influence metrics into client profiles, enabling tailored strategies that align with clients' creative and social capital.

At a broader level, the rise of intangible wealth redefines what society considers valuable and worthy of investment. It challenges entrenched norms privileging material accumulation and calls for more inclusive, multidimensional criteria that embrace human creativity, relationality, and meaning-making. Engaging thoughtfully with this evolution equips professionals and learners to participate in a financial ecosystem that is not only more technologically sophisticated but also more attuned to the diverse ways people generate and perceive value.

In embracing art, expression, and network capital as viable assets, the AI era invites a new alchemy of wealth—one that transforms the abstract into actionable insight, the personal into economic potential, and the social into strategic advantage. This shift is not merely technical but deeply cultural, reshaping financial landscapes and human aspirations alike.

Valuation as a Moral Act –

Valuation, far from being a mere technical exercise confined to balance sheets and market prices, is fundamentally a moral act. Each decision about what to value and how to assign worth reflects a constellation of ethical judgments, cultural norms, and philosophical commitments. This recognition demands a critical reassessment of financial and economic paradigms that often treat value as objective and universally measurable, obscuring the deeper human choices embedded within. By invoking philosophical traditions from Aristotle's concept of the "good life" to John Rawls's theory of justice, this subchapter invites readers to interrogate the assumptions underpinning valuation and to consider the ethical responsibilities that come with defining what matters.

Aristotle's virtue ethics provide a starting point for understanding valuation as inherently tied to human flourishing rather than mere accumulation. For Aristotle, the *telos*—the ultimate purpose—of life is eudaimonia, often translated as flourishing or well-being, achieved through the cultivation of virtues. Applying this lens to financial valuation suggests that metrics prioritising maximum profit or efficiency are insufficient if they neglect the broader context of what constitutes a flourishing life. Wealth, then, is not an end in itself but a means to enable capabilities such as education, health, community participation, and creativity. The moral act of valuation requires alignment with these higher goals, prompting questions about whether current financial systems and AI-driven models serve or undermine human flourishing.

This Aristotelian perspective contrasts sharply with dominant economic frameworks that treat value as reducible to market prices and quantitative indicators like GDP or shareholder returns. Yet, as contemporary thinkers highlight, these measures often fail to capture social goods, environmental sustainability, or psychological well-being. Here, John Rawls's theory of justice as fairness offers a complementary ethical foundation. Rawls argues that a just society structures its institutions so that inequalities benefit the least advantaged and that decisions be made behind a "veil of ignorance," ensuring impartiality. Translating this to valuation compels financial actors and AI systems to embed principles of equity and inclusivity—valuing not only the affluent or efficient but also those marginalised or vulnerable. Valuation becomes a process that can either perpetuate systemic injustice or foster redistributive fairness.

The complexity of valuation deepens when considering how AI systems operationalise worth. Algorithms, often perceived as neutral arbiters, encode the values and biases of their designers, training data, and societal context. For instance, AI models that prioritise short-term returns risk sidelining long-term ecological health or community resilience—values harder to quantify but crucial for intergenerational justice. Moreover, decisions about which data to include or exclude, how to weigh conflicting objectives, and which outcomes to optimise are inherently ethical choices. Recognising AI-driven valuation as a moral act demands transparency and accountability, inviting stakeholders to participate in shaping value frameworks rather than ceding judgment to opaque systems.

Real-world examples illustrate the stakes and possibilities of ethical valuation. Environmental, Social, and Governance (ESG) investing has emerged as a prominent effort to integrate moral values into financial decisions, using AI to assess companies' sustainability practices, labour standards, and governance quality. Yet, critics caution against "greenwashing" and superficial metrics that obscure deeper ethical considerations. Similarly, faith-based investing algorithms tailor portfolios to religious ethical codes, demonstrating how valuation can reflect diverse moral traditions beyond secular utilitarianism. Open-source financial planning models seek to democratise value-setting, enabling communities to co-create norms reflecting their collective priorities.

These cases highlight tensions between standardisation and pluralism in valuation. On one hand, coherent metrics facilitate comparability and scalability; on the other, rigid frameworks risk erasing cultural specificity and individual meaning. Ethical valuation must negotiate this balance, fostering adaptable systems that honour diverse conceptions of value while maintaining integrity and rigor. This requires interdisciplinary engagement among philosophers, economists, technologists, and affected communities.

The philosophical tradition reminds us that valuation is an expression of identity and aspiration as much as calculation. How societies and individuals assign worth reveals their priorities, hopes, and fears. In an age where AI increasingly mediates economic life, the moral imperative is to ensure that these machines reflect and amplify human values rather than supplant them. Valuation becomes a participatory ethical dialogue, not a technocratic decree.

Ultimately, treating valuation as a moral act reframes finance as a profoundly human endeavour. It calls on practitioners, policymakers, and citizens alike to be deliberate and reflective about what they value, how those values are encoded in AI systems, and the consequences of those choices for justice, well-being, and the future of our shared world. This reorientation fosters a financial landscape where worth is measured not solely by profit, but by the richness and dignity of human life.

Chapter 9
Designing a Human-Centered Future

The practice of financial planning is undergoing a quiet but decisive transformation. No longer can it be confined to the sterile task of accumulating wealth or arranging numbers on a ledger. At its most vital, it becomes something more ambitious: an art of life design, a conscious shaping of existence so that money serves meaning, purpose, and values rather than the other way round. In this light, financial strategies are not abstract calculations but instruments for crafting a life that feels coherent, textured, and humane. Artificial intelligence, celebrated so often as finance's disruptive engine, finds itself in an ambiguous role here. Its predictive brilliance and analytic reach are undeniable, but it must remain a partner—an able assistant—not a sovereign force. The true work is still human: creating lives that matter.

Readers are invited into this reframing not as spectators but as participants. For financial planning, approached rightly, is as philosophical as it is technical. It calls for exercises that might be described as "techno-philosophical": structured provocations, scenarios designed to expose moral tensions, to surface trade-offs, to encourage a designer's mindset in a landscape increasingly shaped by AI. These are not empty abstractions. They are tools for sharpening judgement, for learning to weigh freedom against security, risk against stability, legacy against immediacy—each within the evolving story of one's life.

At the heart of this, of course, lies wisdom. A quality resistant to coding, elusive to quantify, yet indispensable. Algorithms may forecast market shifts, rebalance portfolios, even estimate the probability of certain life events. But they cannot fathom the intricacies of grief, the subtleties of moral obligation, or the quiet intuition that comes only with lived experience. Without the ballast of wisdom, predictive systems risk overreach—confining human possibility within the narrow limits of statistical expectation. To preserve freedom and depth, financial planning must insist on the irreplaceable role of human discernment.

The closing invitation of this chapter is a personal one: to write a letter addressed to one's future self. Not as sentimentality, but as a symbolic gesture of co-authorship. It is a reminder that, in navigating an AI-augmented future, we are not passive recipients of preordained scripts but partners in authorship. Machines may calculate, but only we can articulate the values and hopes that give financial choices their meaning. In this partnership, human agency must not only survive—it must thrive.

What emerges, then, is a framework for financial planning that is broader, more human-centred, and ethically attuned. It acknowledges the power of AI while refusing to let technology dictate the terms of life. It urges readers to balance innovation with insight, machine assistance with moral autonomy, fiscal strategy with the deeper fabric of existence. The destination is not merely wealth but a life designed with integrity and imagination—a financial narrative that reflects who we are and what we aspire to become.

Financial Planning as Life Design –

Financial planning has long been tethered to the pursuit of wealth accumulation, framed narrowly as the optimisation of assets and liabilities. Yet, this perspective increasingly appears outdated in a world where the meaning of success extends far beyond numerical balances. *Reimagining financial planning as life design shifts the mission: it becomes less about growing capital and more about sculpting lives of consequence—lives imbued with purpose, coherence, and resilience.* This paradigm invites a broader dialogue about what it means to steward not only money but the very architecture of a flourishing existence. AI's transformative power, often heralded as a disruptor, promises extraordinary capabilities for this new form of planning. Still, it must serve as an enabler rather than the author of life's narrative, complementing human values without erasing the agency at the heart of meaningful choice.

At the core of this shift lies a fundamental question: *What role should financial planners occupy when the objective transcends profit maximisation to encompass human wellbeing and identity formation?* Traditionally, planners have been number-crunchers—calculators of returns, risk, and tax implications. The new framework demands a more expansive competence, integrating insights from psychology, philosophy, and behavioural science. Planners must become curators of possibility, helping individuals map their aspirations, confront trade-offs, and design financial trajectories aligned with personal meaning. AI, with its data-processing prowess and predictive algorithms, offers tools for simulation, scenario analysis, and real-time adjustment. Yet, its outputs remain contingent on the values embedded in design choices and the interpretive faculties of the planner and client alike.

Consider the example of a retirement plan: classical models focus on portfolio optimisation to maximise income streams or capital preservation. Life design repositions the question: How will retirement support not only financial security but ongoing purpose, social connection, and health? AI can simulate a multitude of retirement scenarios, incorporating longevity risk and market volatility. However, *the decision to prioritise volunteerism, part-time work, or creative pursuits during retirement is fundamentally a human judgement, reflecting deeply held values*. This tension underscores a vital truth: *AI excels at computation but cannot adjudicate meaning or ethical considerations*. Human wisdom remains essential in interpreting AI-generated insights and situating them within a client's broader life story.

This recalibration extends to addressing uncertainty and complexity. Life trajectories are inherently nonlinear, shaped by unpredictable events and evolving desires. AI models can incorporate stochastic elements and machine learning to improve forecasts, yet the future remains open-ended. Financial planning as life design embraces this openness, encouraging adaptability and reflective practice rather than rigid adherence to static plans. Here, planners act as facilitators of ongoing dialogue—between the individual, their circumstances, and the tools they employ. AI-generated feedback loops, such as alerts or behavioural nudges, can enhance this process but must be balanced with critical reflection to avoid technological determinism.

Moreover, the ethical dimensions of this reorientation warrant careful attention. If financial planning influences the very composition of a life, then questions of equity, inclusivity, and cultural sensitivity become paramount. AI systems trained on biased data risk perpetuating inequalities, potentially skewing recommendations away from underrepresented groups or unconventional life paths. *A human-centred approach insists on transparency, participatory design, and accountability to ensure that AI serves diverse values rather than narrow economic interests.* The planner's role expands to that of an ethical steward, safeguarding autonomy and fostering empowerment.

Real-world applications illustrate these principles. Platforms integrating AI-powered personal finance tools now increasingly incorporate qualitative inputs—goals around family, legacy, or health—and translate them into quantitative plans. Robo-advisors, once solely focused on risk-adjusted returns, are experimenting with modules that factor in social impact investing or mental wellness budgets. These innovations reflect an emergent trend towards *holistic financial planning that treats money as a means rather than an end.* Yet, the need for human judgement persists, particularly in navigating ambiguities and contextualising data within lived experience.

The challenge ahead is to cultivate planners capable of synthesising technological adeptness with empathetic insight and ethical discernment. Education and professional development must evolve accordingly, integrating interdisciplinary knowledge and fostering skills in narrative competence and systems thinking. Clients, too, require financial literacy that encompasses understanding of AI's potentials and limitations, enabling informed partnership rather than passive consumption. This collaborative dynamic reframes the client-planner relationship as a co-creative endeavour, where technology amplifies rather than replaces human connection.

Ultimately, financial planning as life design reclaims the profoundly human dimensions of finance. It situates money within a broader constellation of values, relationships, and aspirations, recognising that *wealth is not merely measured in currency but in the richness of a well-crafted life.* AI stands as a formidable tool in this enterprise—providing clarity, efficiency, and insight—but its outputs must be harnessed through the lens of human intention. Only then can financial planning transcend calculation to become an act of meaning-making, empowering individuals to navigate complexity with wisdom and courage.

Techno-Philosophical Exercises –

The intersection of technology, ethics, and financial planning presents one of the most profound challenges of our time. As artificial intelligence and machine learning increasingly influence decisions about wealth, risk, and legacy, the imperative to engage critically with the ethical dimensions of these tools grows urgent. *Techno-philosophical exercises* emerge as essential methodologies—deliberate prompts and scenarios designed not merely to inform but to provoke deep reflection, fostering the capacity to navigate trade-offs and ethical dilemmas inherent in modern financial design. These exercises demand from readers a thoughtful engagement that transcends technical mastery, encouraging the integration of values, foresight, and human judgement in the face of complex algorithmic landscapes.

At the core of these exercises lies a tension between automation's promise of optimisation and the irreplaceable nuances of human meaning-making. Financial AI systems operate by processing vast data sets and generating recommendations aligned with predefined objectives. Yet, the *selection of those objectives*—whether to prioritise maximum return, social impact, or intergenerational equity—is profoundly normative. This raises fundamental questions: Who decides what counts as "optimal"? What are the ethical implications of embedding particular values into financial algorithms? And how do planners and clients negotiate these choices in practice? Exercises grounded in such questions compel readers to adopt a meta-perspective, evaluating the assumptions, biases, and trade-offs that undergird ostensibly objective systems.

Consider a scenario in which an AI-powered wealth management platform recommends a portfolio heavily weighted toward fossil fuel investments due to projected short-term gains, despite the client's expressed environmental concerns. The challenge here is multifaceted. Should the algorithm's optimisation yield to the client's values, even if it means sacrificing returns? How transparent must the platform be about the underlying model's priorities? This prompts reflection on the ethics of *algorithmic default settings* and the necessity of human oversight. The scenario invites readers to interrogate the boundaries between efficiency and ethics, autonomy and paternalism—a balance that no purely technical solution can settle.

Beyond value conflicts, techno-philosophical exercises probe the limits of prediction and the management of uncertainty. Financial planning traditionally grapples with risk as probabilistic volatility, but AI introduces new forms of uncertainty tied to data quality, model opacity, and systemic shifts. Imagine a family relying on an AI tool to forecast educational expenses for their children decades ahead. How should planners incorporate the inherent unpredictability of social, technological, and economic change? Should plans prioritise flexibility over rigid optimisation? Such reflections emphasise *design-thinking* principles—encouraging iterative planning, scenario analysis, and resilience building rather than deterministic forecasts. This approach repositions planning as a dynamic dialogue with uncertainty, not a search for certainty.

Ethical reflection also extends to questions of justice and inclusivity. AI systems trained on historical financial data risk replicating systemic biases that disadvantage marginalized groups. Exercises that foreground cases of algorithmic discrimination in lending or wealth assessment compel readers to confront the real-world consequences of neglecting fairness. This invites critical examination of transparency standards, data governance, and the ethical responsibilities of developers and planners. Moreover, readers must grapple with the question of reparative design: How can AI-driven financial tools actively promote equity rather than merely avoid harm? Here, techno-philosophical engagement transcends passive acceptance to embrace proactive stewardship.

The pedagogical power of these exercises lies in their capacity to cultivate ethical literacy alongside technical competence. For instance, a prompt asking readers to devise a financial plan for a client with conflicting short-term needs and long-term goals encourages nuanced prioritisation. It requires the reader to weigh competing values—immediate wellbeing against future security—and to articulate the reasoning behind trade-offs. By simulating such complex decision-making, these exercises build the kind of judgment essential for human-centred financial planning in an AI-mediated world.

A further dimension involves the social and relational aspects of financial ethics. Wealth does not exist in a vacuum; it is embedded within families, communities, and institutions. Exercises that incorporate collective decision-making, intergenerational considerations, or communal wealth pools illuminate the ethical challenges of balancing individual agency with collective responsibility. For example, how should AI tools support family wealth transitions that respect diverse values across generations? What mechanisms ensure that communal financial decisions remain accountable and inclusive? These questions foster a systemic perspective, reinforcing the interconnectedness of financial choices and social dynamics.

Practical application of techno-philosophical exercises also benefits from real-world case studies. The rise of ESG (Environmental, Social, Governance) investing, faith-aligned portfolios, and impact investing illustrates attempts to embed ethics into financial decision-making. Yet, these initiatives frequently confront tensions between quantitative metrics and qualitative values. For example, how does one measure "social good" in a way that is rigorous yet sensitive to context? Exercises based on these cases invite readers to critique existing frameworks and imagine novel approaches that integrate AI's analytical strengths with ethical plurality.

Importantly, these exercises serve not only as intellectual challenges but as invitations to cultivate *moral imagination*—the ability to envision the consequences of financial decisions beyond immediate gains. They provoke questions about legacy, stewardship, and the kind of futures we collectively construct. By engaging with ethical dilemmas through the lens of financial planning, readers are equipped to approach AI not as passive recipients but as active co-creators of technology that reflects human values and aspirations.

In sum, techno-philosophical exercises function as a vital bridge between the mathematical precision of AI and the inherently normative realm of human values. They compel readers to confront the ambiguities and responsibilities of designing financial futures in a world where algorithms exert unprecedented influence. Through critical reflection, scenario analysis, and ethical deliberation, these exercises deepen understanding and sharpen the capacity to harness

AI for *financial planning that honours both efficiency and humanity.* They reaffirm that while AI can illuminate pathways, the ultimate direction must emerge from human wisdom and moral courage.

The Role of Wisdom –

The promise of artificial intelligence to revolutionise financial planning rests heavily on its unparalleled ability to analyse vast datasets, identify patterns, and predict outcomes with precision. Yet, amid this era of predictive overreach, a crucial question emerges: *What is lost when we privilege data-driven forecasts over human wisdom?* The role of wisdom—intuitive, experiential, and deeply contextual—remains indispensable, not only as a counterbalance to algorithmic certainty but as a guiding force in navigating the ethical, emotional, and existential dimensions of financial decision-making. This subchapter asserts that preserving and elevating human insight within the AI-infused landscape is not a nostalgic impulse but a vital necessity for fostering meaningful, resilient financial lives.

At first glance, AI's predictive capacities appear to offer a panacea for uncertainty, promising to optimise investment returns, manage risk, and tailor financial plans with unprecedented granularity. However, *prediction is inherently probabilistic,* subject to the vagaries of incomplete data, shifting contexts, and unforeseen events. Here, the limitations of even the most sophisticated models become evident: they can map the contours of past and present but struggle to anticipate the nuances of human values, aspirations, or moral dilemmas. Wisdom, in contrast, embodies the capacity to interpret uncertainty, synthesise disparate inputs, and apply ethical judgement, often drawing upon tacit knowledge and lived experience inaccessible to machines.

Consider the example of retirement planning. AI algorithms can calculate the statistically optimal savings rate or asset allocation based on historical market trends and life expectancy data. Yet, a human planner's wisdom accounts for the client's unique life narrative—the desire to support ageing parents, to travel extensively in later years, or to engage in community philanthropy. Such aspirations may defy neat quantification but profoundly shape what "success" means for that individual. Here, wisdom acts as a *translator between numbers and narratives*, enabling financial plans that resonate with clients' deeper sense of purpose rather than mere portfolio performance.

The preservation of wisdom also encompasses emotional intelligence, a realm where AI's capabilities remain embryonic. Financial decisions are rarely dispassionate; they intersect with identity, fear, hope, and trust. Research consistently shows that clients value empathy, reassurance, and the nuanced understanding of their circumstances—qualities that foster adherence to financial plans even in volatile markets. A planner's wisdom includes recognising moments when data-driven advice must be tempered with human compassion and when behavioural nudges may need adjustment to avoid undue anxiety or complacency. In this light, *wisdom is not opposed to technology but enriches its application*, ensuring that AI augments rather than supplants the human dimension.

Philosophically, the role of wisdom recalls classical traditions from Aristotle's concept of *phronesis*—practical wisdom aimed at achieving the good life—to contemporary reflections on moral judgement in complex systems. Aristotle distinguished wisdom from mere knowledge by emphasising deliberation, context-sensitivity, and virtue. Translating this to financial planning underscores the imperative to engage with clients not as data points but as whole persons embedded in social and temporal webs. As AI accelerates the quantification of financial life, wisdom demands vigilance against reducing value solely to measurable outputs, urging planners to safeguard holistic, ethical perspectives.

This philosophical grounding gains urgency in light of AI's propensity to amplify existing biases and systemic inequities. Algorithms, trained on historical data, may inadvertently reinforce discriminatory lending or investment practices. Wisdom here manifests as *critical oversight*, the capacity to interrogate and challenge algorithmic outputs rather than accepting them as neutral truths. Human insight is required to identify when models perpetuate injustice, to advocate for transparency, and to champion fairness in financial ecosystems. This protective role illustrates wisdom's function as a moral compass amidst technological complexity.

Furthermore, wisdom is indispensable in navigating *ambiguity and emergent risks*—those threats and opportunities that defy prediction due to novelty or rapid change. Climate change, geopolitical instability, and technological disruption exemplify challenges where reliance on past data alone is inadequate. Wise financial planning embraces *adaptive resilience*, cultivating strategies that maintain flexibility and responsiveness rather than fixating on optimisation under static assumptions. This entails fostering a mindset of humility and curiosity, recognising the limits of foresight while preparing for multiple plausible futures.

The integration of wisdom with AI also shapes the evolving identity and role of financial professionals. As routine calculations become increasingly automated, planners must cultivate distinctively human skills: ethical reasoning, storytelling, and the facilitation of meaning-making. Wisdom enables them to interpret AI-generated insights critically, to contextualise recommendations, and to engage clients in co-creative processes of financial life design. This shift from transactional advice to relational stewardship highlights wisdom as both a personal and professional imperative.

Educational paradigms likewise must evolve to foreground wisdom alongside technical proficiency. Financial literacy should include *ethical reflection*, scenario analysis, and experiential learning that prepare future planners and clients to exercise judgement under uncertainty. This broader conception acknowledges that effective financial decision-making transcends algorithms and requires cultivation of character, discernment, and dialogue.

In sum, the ascendancy of AI in financial planning heralds transformative possibilities but also profound risks of reductive thinking and mechanistic control. *Wisdom—rooted in human insight, ethical reflection, and emotional intelligence—remains the indispensable counterweight*, ensuring that financial lives are crafted not merely through predictive algorithms but through thoughtful, compassionate engagement with complexity and meaning. The challenge before us is not to resist technological progress but to harness it in ways that amplify rather than eclipse the wisdom that defines our humanity.

A Letter to the Future Self –

The notion of writing a letter to one's future self might seem, at first, a sentimental exercise, yet in the context of today's AI-augmented financial landscape, it emerges as a profound act of agency and co-creation. This subchapter invites readers to transcend the passive role of recipients in an algorithmically curated future and instead become active architects alongside artificial intelligence. In doing so, it reframes financial planning from a static projection into a dynamic dialogue—one that blends human intention with machine insight to shape futures that are not only prosperous but profoundly meaningful. The imperative is clear: to approach AI not as a deterministic force but as a collaborative partner in life design.

At its core, the letter to the future self is an exercise in intentionality. It demands the reader to articulate values, aspirations, and uncertainties at this precise moment, projecting them forward into a yet unwritten narrative. This act of self-address serves as a grounding counterweight to the vast, often impersonal data streams that AI processes. While algorithms excel at identifying patterns and predicting probabilities, they lack the capacity to hold one's evolving sense of purpose or to wrestle with the moral complexities embedded in life choices. *By composing a letter to the future self, individuals embed their own voice into the planning process—humanising and contextualising what might otherwise become a cold calculus.*

The practical dimension of this exercise is illuminated by emerging AI-driven tools that enable personalised, scenario-based planning. Platforms now allow users to simulate diverse financial futures based on different assumptions and behavioural patterns, offering unprecedented visibility into the consequences of today's decisions. Yet, the decision to act on these insights remains fundamentally human. The letter to the future self anchors this process by encouraging reflection on *which possibilities resonate* with one's values and which trade-offs are acceptable. This blend of reflective writing and AI-driven modelling cultivates a partnership: machines provide clarity and foresight, while humans provide judgement and meaning.

Such co-authorship challenges the often binary framing of human versus machine capabilities. Rather than ceding control or resisting automation, embracing AI as a partner requires cultivating new literacies—technological fluency coupled with ethical discernment and self-awareness. This necessitates an ongoing dialogue, not a one-off interaction. Future selves are not distant spectators but participants in a continuous feedback loop, where intentions are revisited and recalibrated in light of new data and lived experience. *The letter is thus both a prompt and a living document, inviting iterative engagement and adaptability.*

However, this partnership entails navigating inherent tensions. One such tension lies in balancing trust and scepticism towards AI's recommendations. Trust arises from transparency, explainability, and demonstrable alignment with one's goals, yet blind faith risks abdication of responsibility. The letter to the future self becomes a tool of empowerment, prompting questions: *Does this plan reflect my authentic priorities? What values might be eclipsed by algorithmic optimisation? How do I remain accountable to myself and my community?* These questions underscore the moral dimension of co-creating with AI, emphasising that technology is not neutral but embedded with assumptions and biases requiring vigilant scrutiny.

Another tension concerns the unpredictability of life itself. AI models, however advanced, cannot fully anticipate black swan events, shifting societal norms, or transformations in personal identity. The letter to the future self acknowledges this uncertainty by embracing humility and openness. It invites the reader to envision multiple potential selves and futures, recognising that financial planning must be resilient and flexible rather than rigidly prescriptive. This anticipatory stance aligns with design-thinking principles that value prototyping, experimentation, and learning from failure—a mindset essential for navigating complexity.

Philosophically, the practice of addressing one's future self resonates with concepts of narrative identity and temporal agency. Drawing from thinkers such as Charles Taylor and Paul Ricoeur, identity is understood not as fixed but as a continuously unfolding story. Financial plans, when co-authored with AI, become chapters in this story rather than isolated forecasts. The letter acts as a bridge between present intentions and future realities, inviting dialogue across time that honours both continuity and change. It transforms financial planning from a technical exercise into a deeply human project of self-realisation and legacy.

Real-world applications of this approach are already surfacing in innovative financial wellness programmes. For example, certain robo-advisors integrate reflective prompts alongside algorithmic advice, encouraging users to contextualise recommendations within their broader life goals. Similarly, some wealth management firms are incorporating narrative coaching and digital journaling as complementary practices to quantitative analysis. These initiatives recognise that fostering a sense of ownership and meaning in financial planning enhances both satisfaction and adherence, ultimately leading to more sustainable outcomes.

The letter to the future self also invites communal dimensions. While inherently personal, these reflections can be shared within families or advisory relationships, fostering intergenerational dialogue and collective wisdom. AI can support this by aggregating and translating diverse perspectives into coherent scenarios that respect individual and shared aspirations. This communal co-creation mitigates the isolation often experienced in financial decision-making and cultivates trust through transparency and shared understanding.

In embracing the role of co-author with AI, readers reclaim agency in shaping not only their financial destinies but the ethical contours of the AI systems themselves. By articulating intentions clearly and reflecting critically on algorithmic suggestions, individuals participate in a feedback loop that can influence design and governance of financial technologies. This participatory stance aligns with broader calls for democratizing AI, ensuring it serves human flourishing rather than narrow metrics of efficiency or profit.

Ultimately, the letter to the future self is a call to action—a reminder that the future is neither preordained nor solely machine-generated but co-constructed through human insight, creativity, and responsibility. It beckons readers to step out of passivity, to engage actively with the promises and perils of AI, and to author financial lives imbued with meaning and resilience. This partnership, grounded in reflective intentionality and iterative learning, offers a hopeful vision for navigating complexity with wisdom and purpose.

Conclusion
The Final Asset

Legacy is too often reduced to a ledger of possessions—a house, a portfolio, a set of numbers on paper. But to leave something behind has never been so simple, and in the age of artificial intelligence it becomes even less so. Wealth, in its truest sense, is not confined to property deeds or bank accounts. It is inscribed in the choices we make, the algorithms we train, the values we encode into systems that will long outlast us. These technologies carry forward not just capital but a worldview, a pattern of priorities through which future generations will learn to navigate their own lives. Here, legacy reveals itself less as inheritance and more as meaning: a complex bequest etched into the architectures we design and the ethics we choose to uphold.

The point cannot be postponed to a tidy epilogue. The responsibility is already upon us. Every predictive model, every automated adviser, every wealth management platform quietly embeds decisions—some deliberate, others unintended. These artefacts will structure the possibilities of those who follow, shaping their vulnerabilities and their horizons of prosperity. It is worth asking, then, with some seriousness: what legacies are we in fact engineering? To answer requires not only technical brilliance but moral clarity, for we are constructing the scaffolding of intergenerational wealth and wisdom in tandem.

The ambivalence many feel toward AI—swinging between awe at its prowess and dread of its reach—cannot be the end state. What is needed is not passive acceptance or blanket rejection but conscious participation. We must engage as co-authors, steering rather than surrendering, treating AI neither as master nor as menace but as collaborator. This is perhaps the most enduring asset we might cultivate: the ability to shape technologies through responsibility, imagination, and care.

To do so calls for a subtle but profound shift—from mastery to maturity. Mastery implies domination, the urge to command and conquer. Such rhetoric suited the industrial age but falters in the face of systems as complex and unpredictable as today's algorithms. Maturity, by contrast, is grounded in patience, discernment, and ethical attentiveness. It acknowledges uncertainty as unavoidable, prediction as fallible, and human judgement as indispensable. In this reframing, AI is no longer simply a machine for accumulation but a teacher of restraint, a prompt to balance efficiency with significance.

Thus the chapter extends its hand as an invitation rather than a conclusion: reflect on what values you are encoding into the financial tools you build or adopt; recognise that algorithmic inheritance is real and already unfolding; and embrace the possibility of co-creation where human wisdom and machine intelligence converse rather than collide. A legacy, seen this way, is not a static monument but a living system, shifting and evolving with each generation that inherits and reinterprets it.

This vision also demands vigilance. The risk is clear: if left unchecked, financial AI will reproduce inequities already entrenched, optimising for short-term gain while eroding long-term justice. To counter this, we must learn to weave principles of fairness, care, and responsibility into the very fabric of code and policy. And beyond fairness, there is empathy—the ability to imagine how today's decisions reverberate across decades, affecting lives and communities far removed from our immediate sight.

In closing, the argument circles back to a truth that ought never be lost: finance, stripped to its essence, is about life. It is about the conditions under which people thrive, the narratives we choose to hand down, the futures we allow ourselves to believe are possible. Legacy, therefore, is both material and immaterial, a balance sheet of values and relationships as much as of assets.

What remains for the reader is not merely a summary of arguments but a framework for agency. It is a call to become a discerning navigator in a world where AI presses forward regardless of our readiness. To accept this charge is to see legacy not as the end of a story but as its beginning—a stage on which questions of inheritance, co-evolution, and human purpose are played out in new, unfolding forms.

The Wealth We Leave Behind –

Legacy, traditionally understood as the material wealth transferred across generations, now demands a more expansive interpretation. In an age shaped by pervasive algorithms, artificial intelligence, and digital economies, the wealth we leave behind extends far beyond financial statements and property deeds. *It becomes a complex inheritance of meaning, values, and systemic imprints—intangible assets that will frame the lives and choices of future generations.* This article embarks on a meditation about legacy not as mere money, but as the enduring influence encoded in the systems we build and the ethical frameworks we embed within them. It interrogates what it means to leave behind wealth that is as much about wisdom, context, and agency as it is about currency.

Our choices today—especially those manifested in algorithmic design, data curation, and AI deployment—constitute legacies that transcend conventional inheritance. They shape the *architecture of opportunity*, affecting access to credit, education, healthcare, and civic participation for decades to come. Unlike tangible wealth, these legacies are often invisible, distributed across codebases and decision trees, yet their consequences are concrete and far-reaching. For example, consider predictive models used in credit scoring: biases embedded in training data can inadvertently perpetuate structural inequities, skewing financial inclusion for descendants of marginalised communities. Thus, *the ethical responsibility of today's decision-makers encompasses stewardship of not only assets but of fairness, dignity, and future possibility.*

The notion of legacy as meaning invites a reevaluation of what we prioritise in wealth transmission. It challenges the reduction of inheritance to material gain and presses us to recognise *values, narratives, and social capital as crucial components* of intergenerational wealth. In practical terms, this means considering how family stories, cultural knowledge, and shared aspirations are preserved or transformed through digital platforms. Emerging technologies now facilitate the curation of "living legacies"—interactive repositories where context, intention, and wisdom accompany financial documents. These innovations suggest that *wealth is no longer static but dynamically co-authored between generations, mediated by AI that can encode and transmit ethos alongside assets.*

Yet this transformation poses critical tensions. The increasing automation of financial decisions risks obscuring human judgement and ethical nuance beneath layers of algorithmic opacity. If legacy is to encompass more than cold calculation, then human values must remain central to the design and interpretation of AI systems. This demands transparency, explainability, and participatory governance models that empower communities to shape the futures inscribed by technology. *Legacy thus becomes a collective project, negotiated not only within families but across societal boundaries, influenced by public policy and ethical deliberation.*

At a philosophical level, this shift prompts us to reconsider wealth as a multi-dimensional construct, integrating emotional, cultural, and moral dimensions with economic measures. Drawing from traditions that emphasise virtue and the common good—from Aristotle's notion of *eudaimonia* to Rawls's principles of justice—we are urged to expand the metrics by which we assess legacy. What does it mean to leave a world richer not just in capital but in *justice, meaning, and human flourishing*? How can AI tools be harnessed to support such aspirations rather than undermine them? These questions demand both critical reflection and creative imagination.

Several real-world initiatives illustrate this evolving paradigm. Platforms that blend financial planning with narrative tools enable clients to document their values, hopes, and lessons alongside wealth transfer plans. Blockchain-based "smart wills" offer programmable inheritance that enforces ethical stipulations and charitable giving automatically, ensuring that legacy reflects intention as much as asset allocation. Meanwhile, data cooperatives empower individuals and communities to collectively own and monetise their digital footprints, counterbalancing corporate control and fostering equitable wealth creation. These examples signal a movement toward legacy as *active, ethical, and participatory design* rather than passive inheritance.

Nevertheless, this broadened understanding of legacy does not negate the importance of material wealth; rather, it situates financial assets within a richer ecosystem of inheritance. It underscores that the *true currency of legacy is the quality of life and relational fabric we enable for those who follow.* How AI shapes this fabric—through decisions encoded in automated systems, through the curation or erasure of cultural memory, and through the governance of shared resources—will be a defining ethical frontier of our time.

The stewardship of this new form of wealth demands an integrative approach, combining technological literacy with philosophical insight, legal foresight, and social empathy. Professionals across disciplines must collaborate to ensure that the legacies inscribed by AI reflect pluralistic values and support resilient, just communities. This means moving beyond reductive metrics of financial success and embracing *a holistic vision of legacy as layered, evolving, and deeply human.*

In sum, the wealth we leave behind is no longer solely measured by ledgers but by the enduring influence of our choices—algorithms that govern access, narratives that preserve meaning, and values that guide equity. As readers of this work engage with the technologies and ideas presented throughout, they are invited to see themselves as *co-creators of legacies that matter*, architects not only of wealth but of the world that wealth enables. This recognition challenges us to act with foresight, responsibility, and hope, conscious that the final inheritance is as much about the lives we help shape as the fortunes we bequeath.

Choosing with Eyes Open –

The accelerating integration of artificial intelligence into every facet of financial life confronts us with a defining choice: to approach AI with fear, blind reverence, or conscious agency. *Choosing with eyes open is no longer a philosophical ideal but an urgent imperative.* The stakes extend beyond individual portfolios and market trends to the very architecture of trust, equity, and human flourishing in a technologically mediated world. This article asserts that responsible, creative, and ethical co-evolution with AI must replace passive consumption or dystopian fatalism. It challenges readers to move beyond simplistic binaries—of AI as either saviour or threat—and instead embrace a nuanced, participatory relationship that preserves human dignity and amplifies collective wisdom.

The allure of AI lies in its promise to optimise decisions, predict risks, and unlock efficiencies previously unimaginable. Yet this promise is inseparable from profound risks: algorithmic bias, privacy erosion, concentration of power, and the potential hollowing out of human judgement. *A critical insight is that AI does not operate in a vacuum; it reflects the values, assumptions, and power dynamics embedded by its creators and users.* Thus, every AI deployment in finance is an ethical act with downstream effects on inclusion, autonomy, and social justice. Recognising this compels us to move beyond passive acceptance towards informed scrutiny and proactive shaping of these technologies.

Central to conscious participation is understanding the *trade-offs inherent in AI-driven financial systems*. For instance, automated credit scoring may increase access for many but exacerbate disparities for others if training data encodes historical discrimination. Similarly, high-frequency trading algorithms enhance market liquidity but can destabilise systems in flash crashes. These tensions illustrate that technological optimisation rarely aligns perfectly with societal values. Rather than delegating responsibility solely to AI designers or regulators, *users and stakeholders must engage critically with AI outputs, questioning assumptions and demanding transparency*. This shared accountability fosters resilience and mitigates unintended harms.

The creative dimension of co-evolution emphasises *innovation grounded in ethics and human-centric design*. Financial AI tools can be developed not merely to maximise profits but to enhance wellbeing, support sustainable investing, and nurture long-term resilience. Examples include AI platforms that integrate environmental, social, and governance (ESG) criteria into investment decisions or that facilitate personalised financial coaching incorporating psychological insights. These approaches highlight that *ethical AI in finance is not a constraint but a catalyst for richer, more meaningful innovation*—one that honours complexity rather than reducing humans to data points.

Ethical frameworks provide vital guidance in this endeavour, but they are not static prescriptions. *They require continual refinement through dialogue, empirical testing, and cultural sensitivity*. The field of AI ethics, especially in finance, grapples with competing priorities: privacy versus transparency, individual autonomy versus collective good, efficiency versus fairness. Navigating these tensions demands humility and adaptability. Financial professionals, technologists, and users alike must cultivate an *ethics literacy* that empowers them to interpret evolving norms and technologies critically, fostering a culture of reflective practice rather than blind trust.

A particularly pressing concern is the opacity of many AI systems, often described as "black boxes." Without clear explanations of how AI reaches decisions, users risk abdicating judgement, undermining agency. *Explainable AI (XAI) initiatives aim to bridge this gap by making algorithmic reasoning accessible and interpretable*. Yet transparency alone is insufficient; trust must be earned through consistent ethical behaviour, stakeholder engagement, and mechanisms for contestation and redress. Co-evolution entails *building institutional and community infrastructures that support such trust-building practices*, thereby reinforcing democratic values in digital finance.

Real-world case studies illustrate both the promise and pitfalls of choosing with eyes open. The financial technology platform Tala uses AI-driven credit assessments to serve underbanked populations, improving financial inclusion while consciously refining models to reduce bias. Conversely, controversies surrounding facial recognition in loan applications expose how unchecked AI can entrench discrimination. These examples underscore that *ethical AI adoption is neither automatic nor guaranteed; it requires vigilance, iteration, and inclusive governance*. Importantly, they reveal that *users are not powerless* but can influence AI trajectories through demand, feedback, and participation in policy-making.

Moreover, conscious participation must embrace *the creative tensions between human intuition and machine prediction*. While AI excels at processing vast data and identifying patterns, it lacks contextual awareness, moral reasoning, and the ability to imagine futures beyond historical precedent. The best outcomes emerge from hybrid intelligence where *human insight guides and interrogates AI recommendations*, preserving the uniquely human capacities of empathy, judgment, and ethical deliberation. This partnership calls for new literacies—technological fluency coupled with critical thinking and ethical sensitivity.

Ultimately, choosing with eyes open invites us to reconceive our relationship with AI as a dynamic dialogue rather than a unilateral command. It is an ongoing project of co-evolution where *technology shapes society and society shapes technology in return*. This perspective refuses fatalism and triumphalism alike, embracing complexity, uncertainty, and the responsibility of stewardship. Financial actors—whether advisors, regulators, or everyday users—must become proactive custodians of the socio-technical systems they inhabit, *advocating for AI that augments human potential without undermining agency or justice*.

As this definitive guide has sought to demonstrate, the future of finance hinges not on AI alone but on the choices made by those who wield it. To act with eyes open is to engage with AI not as spectators or victims but as partners and co-creators of equitable, resilient, and meaningful financial ecosystems. This entails *embracing both the power and limits of AI, demanding transparency, cultivating ethics, and honouring human wisdom*. It is a call not just to adapt to change but to shape it responsibly—ensuring that the wealth of the future is measured not solely in numbers, but in the depth of trust, fairness, and shared humanity it fosters.

From Mastery to Maturity –

The dominant narrative surrounding artificial intelligence often casts it as a tool to be mastered—an adversary to be conquered or a mechanism to be controlled. Yet this view, while instinctively appealing, is profoundly limited. *Mastery implies domination, certainty, and a linear trajectory toward fixed goals*. It presumes that humans can fully command the complexities of AI, bending it entirely to our will. However, as AI systems become more embedded, autonomous, and interdependent with human decisions, this paradigm begins to fracture. A more compelling and necessary approach is to shift from mastery to maturity: embracing AI as a catalyst for human growth, self-reflection, and ethical evolution rather than mere technical conquest. This article explores how this reorientation challenges prevailing assumptions and offers a richer framework for engaging with AI in financial planning and beyond.

The metaphor of maturity suggests a relationship of coexistence and mutual adaptation rather than unilateral control. It acknowledges that AI will inevitably shape our lives in unpredictable ways, pushing us to develop new capacities—patience with uncertainty, humility before complexity, and a deeper commitment to shared values. This approach reframes AI not as a tool to win more efficiently but as a partner teaching us to become wiser stewards of our resources, communities, and ultimately, our lives. It invites us to cultivate *phronesis*—Aristotle's concept of practical wisdom—where ethical discernment and contextual judgement guide decisions, complementing algorithmic precision.

This shift from mastery to maturity confronts a paradox at the heart of contemporary finance: AI systems excel at optimising for quantifiable outcomes but remain blind to the qualitative nuances that define meaningful human flourishing. For example, predictive analytics can maximise portfolio returns but cannot measure the joy derived from purposeful spending, the comfort of financial security in times of crisis, or the legacy of generosity passed through generations. Maturity demands that financial planning transcend numerical targets, incorporating *ethical reflection and narrative understanding*—domains where human insight remains indispensable.

The increasing complexity and opacity of AI algorithms also underscore the limits of mastery. Many machine learning models operate as "black boxes," with decision pathways too intricate for straightforward explanation. Attempting to assert total control over such systems risks *hubris*—the overconfidence that blinds us to unintended consequences. Instead, maturity calls for *collaborative stewardship*, involving diverse stakeholders in ongoing dialogue, transparency efforts, and the co-creation of ethical guardrails. This participatory ethos mitigates risks while fostering innovation aligned with societal values.

Historical parallels illuminate this transition. The industrial revolution promised mastery over nature through mechanisation but eventually revealed the necessity of *social, ethical, and environmental maturity* to balance progress with wellbeing. Similarly, the AI revolution compels us to move beyond a narrow focus on efficiency and profit toward holistic frameworks that respect dignity, justice, and sustainability. Financial professionals, technologists, and users alike must evolve their skills—not only in technical fluency but in *ethical literacy and emotional intelligence*—to navigate this complex landscape responsibly.

Concrete examples reveal the promise of maturity-oriented AI integration. Consider socially responsible investing platforms that embed ESG metrics alongside financial analysis, encouraging investors to align portfolios with their values rather than merely maximise returns. Or personalised financial coaching apps that integrate behavioural insights to foster resilience and long-term wellbeing. These innovations exemplify *how AI can support wise decision-making without supplanting human judgment*—inviting users into a reflective partnership rather than passive dependence.

Yet embracing maturity is no passive acceptance of AI's trajectory. It requires *active resistance to reductionist narratives* that depict technology as fate or panacea. Maturity means cultivating *critical agency*, recognising AI's profound impact while insisting on human oversight and accountability. This involves grappling with ethical dilemmas, such as balancing privacy with transparency, managing algorithmic biases, and distributing AI's benefits equitably. These challenges demand *continuous learning and moral courage*—hallmarks of mature stewardship.

Moreover, maturity invites us to reconsider what constitutes "winning" in a world shaped by AI. Success shifts from short-term gains and zero-sum competition toward *long-term stewardship, relational harmony, and shared prosperity*. In financial terms, this may mean prioritising stability, inclusion, and the intergenerational transmission of resources and values over volatile speculative gains. Such redefinition requires *patience and a broadened horizon*, qualities that flourish with maturity.

This evolving relationship also reshapes the role of the human expert. Rather than striving for omniscient control, the mature financial advisor becomes a guide and interlocutor—someone who helps clients interpret AI insights, reflect on personal values, and design lives that matter. This role underscores the indispensability of *empathy, narrative competence, and ethical judgement*—dimensions AI cannot replicate. The advisor's wisdom emerges not from predicting every outcome but from fostering *adaptive capacities* in clients facing an uncertain future.

Finally, embracing maturity means seeing AI as a mirror reflecting human aspirations and limitations. It challenges us to confront our biases, fears, and assumptions about control and autonomy. This confrontation can catalyse profound personal and societal growth, encouraging *greater humility, cooperation, and shared responsibility*. In this light, AI becomes a teacher, not merely a tool—guiding us toward *a deeper understanding of what it means to live well* amid complexity.

In reimagining our relationship with AI from mastery to maturity, we open pathways to more resilient, ethical, and fulfilling financial practices. We acknowledge that true wisdom resides not in dominating algorithms but in partnering with them to steward life's richest dimensions. This perspective challenges us to cultivate *enduring virtues—prudence, justice, courage, and temperance*—as the foundation for navigating the AI-inflected financial landscape. Far from diminishing human agency, such maturity expands it, enabling us to author futures marked not by control alone but by meaning, care, and shared flourishing.

About the Author

Eleanor Vale is a thought leader at the intersection of finance, technology, and human well-being. With over a decade of experience studying how emerging technologies reshape human behavior and decision-making, she writes to illuminate the deeper human narratives behind our algorithms. Eleanor's work draws upon behavioral economics, cultural philosophy, and lived experience—from global investment floors to intentional living communities—to explore what it means to lead a life designed, not dictated, by artificial intelligence. Her clear, empathetic voice speaks to both professionals and everyday readers who want to engage with AI not only as a tool, but as a mirror to their values.

www.ingramcontent.com/pod-product-compliance
Lightning Source LLC
Chambersburg PA
CBHW031349230926
51848CB00002B/449
* 9 7 8 9 3 7 1 7 7 9 5 2 4 *